WOMAN AS GOD MADE HER.

The biography of our first parents, as God made them, and described them, before sin ruined them, is very brief and truly suggestive. It is as follows:—

"And Jehovah God created the man in his image; in the image of God created he him; a male and a female created he them. And God blessed them; and God said to them, Be fruitful, and multiply, and fill the earth, and subdue it, and rule over the fish of the sea, and over the fowl of the heavens, and over every living thing that moves on the earth. And God said, Behold, I have given to you every herb scattering seed, which is on the face of all the earth, and every tree, in which is the fruit of a tree scattering seed, to you it shall be given."—Gen. i. 27-30.

"And Jehovah God formed the man of the dust of the ground, and he breathed into his nostrils the breath of life, and the man became a living soul. And Jehovah God planted a garden in Eden, on the east, and there he put the man whom he formed, ... to till it and to keep it. And God commanded the man, saying, Of every tree of the garden thou mayest freely eat. But of the tree of knowledge of good and evil thou shalt not eat of it, for in the day that thou eatest thereof thou shalt surely die. And God said, It is not good that the man should be alone. I will make for him a helper, suited to him. And God caused a deep sleep to fall upon the man, and he slept; and he took one of his ribs, and closed up the flesh in its place. And of this rib which he took from the man, Jehovah God formed a woman, and brought her to the man. And the man said, This now is bone of my bones, and flesh of my flesh. This shall be called Woman, because from man was she taken. Therefore shall a man leave his father and his mother, and shall cleave to his wife; and they shall be one flesh. And they were both naked, the man and his wife, and were not ashamed."—Gen, ii. 7, 8, 15-18, 21-25.

Brief as are these utterances, and familiar as is this language, it is interesting to notice that God has crowded into them every essential fact concerning the origin of woman, the purpose of her creation, and the sphere marked out for her by the Creator's hand.

The simple outline of the story is given us, yet how wonderful is the picture! In the first chapter the origin of man is proclaimed, and his work, "to fill earth and subdue it," is placed before him. In the second chapter, the relation of the sexes is given, and the nature of marriage is explained. What arrests the attention most surely is the resemblance that exists between the experience of our first parents and of their descendants, or between Adam and Eve and ourselves. The "It is not good for man to be alone," spoken by God in Eden, embodies a truth which has lived with the ages, and sets forth an experience felt by every son of Adam. The words "I will make for him a helper suited to him," is man's authority for the faith, that somewhere on the earth God has made a helper suited to him, whom he will recognize, and who will return the recognition. For in all true marriages, now as in Eden, the man and woman do not deliberately seek, but are brought to one another. Happy those who afterwards can recognize that the hand which led his Eve to Adam was that of an invisible God. Man knows that it is not good for him to be alone. Separated from woman's influence, man is narrow, churlish, brutal. Woman is a helper suited to him. With her help he reaches a loftier stature; for love is the very heart of life, the pivot upon which its whole machinery turns, without which no human existence can be complete, and with which it becomes noble and self-sacrificing.

Woman's origin is thus declared:—

"And Jehovah God caused a deep sleep to fall upon the man, and he slept; and he took one of his ribs, and closed up the flesh in its place. And of the rib which he took from the man God formed a woman, and brought her to the man. And the man said, This now is bone of my bones, and flesh of my flesh. This shall be called Woman, because from man was she taken. Therefore shall a man leave his father and his mother, and shall cleave to his wife; and they shall be one flesh."[A] *Woman was taken out of man.* It is man's nature to seek to get her back. He feels that a part of *him* is away from him, until he obtains her. Long years before he sees the woman whom he feels God designed to be his wife, if he be a Christian, believing that she is on the earth, he prays for her weal.

[Footnote A: Gen. ii. 21-24.]

"*Taken out of man!*" How significant these words! Man, without woman, wants completeness—physically, mentally, and spiritually. First, physically. The fact is noticeable that short men often marry tall women, and tall men marry short women. Nervous men marry women who are opposites to them in temperament. This is not a happen so, for that which so often to the unreflecting mind seems unnatural and absurd, to the thinking soul appears as an evidence of God's provident care. Second, mentally. Man desires in his wife that which he lacks. A bookish man seldom desires a wife devoted to the same branch of literature, unless she works as a helpmeet. In taste and in sentiment there must be harmony without rivalry. They must bring products to the common garner, gathered from varying pursuits and from different fields of thought. In music the same law rules. Man, from his very nature, finds in woman a helper in song. Their voices blend in harmony, and give volume, symphony, and variety to the melody produced. Jenny Lind married her assistant, because in sympathy they were one. He was essential to her womanly strength, and without her, he was a mere cipher in the musical world. Together they were a power, felt and acknowledged.

A man full of thought and of genius requires for a wife, not only one who can understand his moods and enjoy his creations, but one who is content to take care of the home, and, perhaps, to manage the business affairs; while many a woman of genius and ability links her fortunes with a plain and appreciative husband, who gladly affords her every means in his power to work in her special sphere. When the wife refuses to act thus wifely, because of her talent, the happiness of the home is imperilled, and the children suffer quite as much, comparatively, as they do in those manufacturing neighborhoods where the wife forsakes the home for the shop, and gives up the vocation of woman to do the work which belongs to man. God made them male and female. He fitted each for separate duties, not for the same duties. Each fills a sphere when each discharges the duties enjoined upon them by their Creator and by society. Wonderful women there are; few of them care to duplicate their power. They prefer to obtain by marriage that which they have not, and which must be supplied by material from without. Homely people oftentimes find beautiful ones to mate them. The rugged seeks the weak. The nervous, the lymphatic. Counterpart that which makes itself complete. This tendency to assimilate is often carried to extremes, because all naturally love that which they possess, and come to prize highly those who regard it with favor. Hence, poor men sometimes marry rich wives, and seldom fail to give something in return. The story is familiar of the two foppish young men who were said to have met at a noted hotel or on change, when one accosted the other by the question, "Who did you marry?" "Ah," said he, "I married fifty thousand dollars. I forget her other name." Such men, however, are exceptions to the rule. There are brainless creatures called men, who will marry a pretty face, though the heart and brain be uncultured, provided there be associated with her sufficient of this world's goods to gratify a mercenary ambition; but the majority, both of men and women, wisely prefer to marry money in a partner rather than money with a partner. The world has a profound contempt for shallow, fussy, empty people, no matter what positions they may occupy.

All sympathize with the rebuke administered to a so-called lady of quality by a Quaker gentleman, who occupied a seat near her in a public coach. She wore an elegant lace shawl, and was dressed to the top of the fashion, but was suffering from the cold. Shivering and shaking, she inquired, "What shall I do to get warm?" "*Thee had better put on another breastpin,*" answered old Broadbrim. The rebuke was timely. Woman degrades herself when she surrenders to fashion that which helps the woman, and which aids her in securing the confidence, the friendship, the respect, and admiration of sensible men.

The truth embodied in the words, "This shall be called Woman, because *from man was she taken*" sheds light upon many a mysterious chapter in life, reconciles the union of contraries in accordance with the law of God, and fills wide realms of life with the radiance of hope, which otherwise would remain mantled in perpetual gloom. If we depended upon those who are like ourselves to sympathize with us, and gird us with strength, we should utterly fail. Oaks cannot lend support to oaks. The vine can do this for the oak, and the oak can give support to the vine; but an oak cannot give strength to its kindred while fulfilling the functions of its life. The same law rules in the mental world. Genius seldom applauds genius, working in its own realm. Very likely it loathes it. The tributes paid to labor are given by the soft-handed rather than by the hard-handed sons of toil. This principle lies back of the appreciation, the commendation, and the support rendered by the different classes of a community to each other.

The God-given and Christ-restored thought of equality between the sexes is seen in the household partnership, where the woman looks for a "smart, but kind" husband, the man for a "capable, sweet-tempered" wife. The man furnishes the house, the woman regulates it. Their relation is one of mutual esteem, mutual dependence. Their talk is of business; their affection shows itself by practical kindness. They know that life goes more smoothly and cheerfully to each for the other's aid; they are grateful and content. The wife praises her husband as a "good provider;" the husband, in return, compliments her as a capital housekeeper. This relation is good as far as it goes; but the heart of the man or woman is unsatisfied, if to household partnership intellectual companionship be not added.

Men can hire their houses kept. Love cannot be purchased. Soul communion is the gift of God. It is very often enjoyed on earth. Men engaged in public life, literary men and artists, have often found in their wives companions and confidants in thought, no less than in feeling. And as the intellectual development of woman has spread wider and risen higher, they have, not unfrequently, shared the same employments.

Thirdly, spiritual. The highest grade of marriage union is the spiritual, which may be expressed as a pilgrimage towards a common shrine.

There is something in every man which he feels to be the essential thing about him. This it is which he desires to have loved. Neglect what else you choose, you must not neglect that. It is the spiritual part of man,—the God-given characteristic which longs for sympathy. Men feel that this want has been met when they say, "Such a one understands me, knows me, sees me, is in sympathy with me." Such moments are to all of priceless value. Whoever meets this want is a boon from God. No matter what the complexion, nor how the features seem: soul meets soul. The heart feels a new life. The union is formed. *Call it affinity, or what you will*, they love in one another the future good which they aid one another to unfold. This includes home sympathies and household wisdom. Such fellowship makes of home a joy, and of toil a delight. When first the joy is reached, a foretaste of heaven is enjoyed. "For it is the one rift of heaven which makes all heaven appear possible; the ecstasy of hope and faith, out of which grows the love which is our strongest mortal instinct and intimation of immortality."

Women are as conscious of this feeling as are men. There are times when women meet their counterpart. The nature they long for and seek after with unutterable longing, is before them. Finding it, they recognize their lord, under whose protection they take shelter, and to whose rule they submit, because of love which masters and controls them. The heart cries out for a person—not for things. Spirit desires spirit; soul yearns for soul. It is the genius of woman to be electrical in movement, intuitive in penetration, and spiritual in tendency. She excels not so easily in classification or recreation as in an instinctive seizure of causes, and a simple breathing out of what she receives, that has the singleness of life, rather than the selecting and energizing of art. More native is it to her to be the living model of the artist, than to set apart from herself any one form in objective reality. More native to inspire and receive the poem than to create it. In so far as soul is in her completely developed, all soul is the same; but in so far as it is modified in her as woman, it flows, it breathes, it sings, rather than deposits soil, or furnishes work; and that which is especially feminine, flushes in blossom the face of the earth, and pervades, like air and water, all this seeming solid globe, daily renewing and purifying its life. Such is the especial feminine element which man desires as a helper, and which is suited to him, and which compels him to exclaim, "O, my God, give it to me *for mine*!"

It is said, "A woman will sometimes idealize a very inferior man, until her love for him exalts him into something better than he originally was, and her into little short of an angel; but a man almost invariably drops to the level of the woman he is in love with. He cannot raise her; but she can almost unlimitedly deteriorate him." This was true of Adam. Eve, sinning, brought him to her level. Why this should be, Heaven knows; but so it constantly is. We have but to look around us, with ordinary observation, in order to see that a man's destiny, more than even a woman's, depends far less upon the good or ill fortune of his wooing than upon the sort of woman with whom he falls in love.

Before a man loves, he is under obligations to himself, to his future, and to the world, to ask himself, Is this woman suited to me? Will she help me to fulfil my mission? Does she supply my want? Can I recognize her as God's gift to me? If Yes, then he is right in loving; for

"He either fears his fate too much,
  Or his deserts are small,
Who dares not put it to the touch,
  And win or lose it all."

A woman, writing of woman, has truly said, "There are but two ways open to any woman. If she loves a man, and he does not love her, to give him up may be a horrible pang and loss; but it cannot be termed a sacrifice: she resigns what she never had. But if he does love her, and she knows it, and if she loves him, she has a right, in spite of the whole world, to hold to him till death do them part. She is bound to marry him, though twenty other women loved him, and broke their hearts in loving him. He is not theirs, but hers; and to have her for his wife is his right and her duty." "And in this world are so many contradictory views of duty and exaggerated notions of light, so many false sacrifices and remunerations, weak even to wickedness, that it is but fair sometimes to uphold the right of love,—love sole, absolute, and paramount,—firmly holding its own, and submitting to nothing and no one, except the laws of God and righteousness." Well and truthfully spoken. Lift up this principle, and behold how it showers benedictions upon all classes and upon all men.

Much is said against amalgamation, as though it were a crime. There is no crime in it or about it. There is much of prejudice, but no crime. Soul marries soul. If a white man loves the soul of a black woman, there is no law in God's code forbidding the union. God made of one blood all nations of men to dwell on all the face of the earth. Complexions may differ, owing to climate, or temperament, but the blood is the same. The race has a common Father in God.

In this intermingling of races, coming to this land from all climes, we perceive the seedling of a glorious hope. The future American is to be the product of this blending of the distinctive features of all the various nations of earth.

Against this result there is an immense amount of prejudice, born of slavery; but in Europe it does not exist, nor is it in fact so universal in this land as many suppose. Many a white man has found his helpmeet in a black woman, and many more will find helpmeets from the same source.

2. "*Woman was taken out of man*." There is significance in the locality from which she was taken. Not from the superior part, that she might think herself superior to man, or endowed with the right to rule him. Her sin consisted in her failing to recognize the position assigned. She was created an associate and an equal, and acted independently, and as an adviser. She took advantage of her position as wife, and became an ally of Satan.

She was not taken from an inferior portion of his body, that he might think her inferior to himself, and to be trampled on by him, but out of his side,—from his rib,—that she might appear to be equal to him; and from a part near his heart, and under his arm, to show that she should be affectionately loved by him, and be always under his care and protection.

Wherever man has failed to recognize this truth society has gone back to barbarism, and the very conception of a home has been banished from the mind. In the East man rules woman as lord. She is his slave; and in the Arabic language there is no word meaning "home." Christian civilization lifts woman up, and thrones her in the heart of a *home*.

She was made from "bone and flesh,"—quickened dust,—and so in her make and constitution she is of superior quality and of finer mould.

The Hebrew word translated "made," means *built*. From the rib God built this woman. How instructive the fact! Woman added to man is the foundation of the home or family. She is built out of man. Man is necessary to her development. A man can continue the work begun by God. He can build up a woman; and as he builds her up he builds up himself. She is also a builder. She builds up a home, or degrades it. If woman is honored in a home, she makes it honorable.

At the outset she was man's equal: perhaps she may have thought herself to be superior to him—more refined, of better material. She forgot her place, and ignored her sphere, and lost all. She was not created as things were, out of nothing. She was meant to be something better than a *thing*; and she must be something better than a thing, or she is nothing. She was not formed as Adam was, out of the dust of the earth. Had she been, perhaps she would not have disliked dust so terribly. She is a part of man's life. This describes her mission. The life of a woman who does not care to be a man's toy or ornament, but desires rather to be his helpmeet,—supplying all he needs, as he supplies all she needs,—is but the continuance, the flowing out and flowing on of man's higher life, into the flowers of love, which decorate the home, and make that chosen retreat the very portals of heaven.

As man feels that in woman he finds the complement to himself, and almost his other self, woman finds in man the same complement to herself, and recognizes in him the ruler of her life, her friend, her lover; and happy is she if she finds in him her husband, who rightfully assumes his rights and his sovereignty.

3. "*God brought her unto man.*" Woman is God's first gift to man. She must never occupy a second place. In the heart she holds a first place, or she holds none at all. The moment she holds a secondary place she is ruined. It is in her power to hold the first place. To do this, she must prize it; make sacrifices to keep it; almost, at times, deny herself, and bear a cross, to hold on to it. Yet it is hers, and God will see to it that she maintains her right.

"*God brought her.*" Every husband in this world should feel that his wife is God's gift to him, and it is his duty to study its characteristics, and minister to them. Every man can make the partner of his life a good wife, and can feel that she was God-given, and must be used in such a manner that when the day of reckoning comes, he can give a good account of the manner in which he has used this blessing. To go to the judgment, and meet a broken-hearted woman, over whom man has exercised tyranny, and to whom he has been a monster, until hope died, and the grave became a refuge, will not be a pleasant meeting.

In this bestowal of woman upon man, we recognize two facts.

1. The father's right to give away his child—a right which exerts its influence at the present time, and which every young man who seeks properly the hand of woman is compelled to recognize. In that act of Eden lie the rule and example to be followed by parents and children: the one to

dispose of their children, and the other to have the consent of their parents in reaching conclusions upon which hinges the destiny of the individual for time, and perhaps for eternity. Happy the child that trusts a wise parent, and refuses to walk a path over which the shadow of parental disapproval rests! Happy the parent who finds pleasure in the fresh young love of the child, and watches the opening flower and the ripening fruit with pride and pleasure.

This giving away of the child requires the enjoyment of perfect confidence between father and daughter and mother and son.

God knew Eve, for he built her. He knew her heart, her mind, her aspiration. A parent knows something of the child; and well it is for both parent and child when this knowledge is perfect, and when the relation subsisting between parents and children is such that home is a place of consultation. A home without secrets, without closed doors, and locked drawers and sugar-boxes,—a home where thought is free, and mind is untrammelled, is the very gate of heaven.

There are homes where the children are excluded from counsel, from love, from plan, from association. Those children live in a world apart from their parents, and it will not be strange if they are swept out by the waves of evil to ruin.

There are homes where the father shuts himself away from the wife and children. To the children he is harsh, unsympathetic, and morose. Ah! there is sorrow in that house. The mother—God bless her!—has a hard time. She has to keep in with the father, and she will keep in with the children. In that bundle of life the tendrils of her nature are bound up. She fights a prolonged battle in regard to expenditure and education. Happiness only comes when the household is one, and the relations between father and children are perfect, as God designed them to be.

Again, God gives his sanction not only to the truth that man's wants can only be met by the gift of woman,—a fact which every man has felt, and which causes every man to feel that somewhere on earth his wife is living, who will recognize and welcome him to the bliss of love and to the joy of companionship,—but this additional truth is taught: Man has a right to marry. Love is no disgrace. It is the pretence of it, for base purposes, which is disgraceful. The nuptial vow was first whispered in the garden. God was sponsor, and all Eden witnesses. This bond of union was God's gift to the race. The curse did not touch it. The marriage vow and marriage rite, with the faith in woman as a helpmeet, have survived the fall, and are our joy and rejoicing at this time.

In conclusion, think of God's care for man, in providing woman as a blessing. There is no necessity for man's being alone. Some one waits to bless or has blessed him. Let us make more of our wives and sisters than ever before. Let us build them up in love and in those generous qualities which fit woman for her high destiny in this fallen world.

2. Think, woman, of your noble mission. You are to be a help to man. You are to help him morally and spiritually. For this God created you. For this he preserves you. "You are queens and bondmaids too, as royal when you serve as when you rule." Man must respect you, for when man loses his respect for woman he is lost. He goes down, down to irremediable ruin. With woman as God designed her, man gets much of Eden back, for in Christ she is reconciled to God. It is for man and woman to get back Eden. Christ came to be our common helper. He is woman's Saviour as well as man's, and offers to all that help which changes life's desert into a garden, and life's gloom into the brilliancy of an eternal day.

"Hail, woman! Hail, thou faithful wife and mother,
The latest, choicest part of heaven's great plan.

None fills thy peerless place at home, no other
   Helpmeet is found for laboring, suffering man.
Hail, thou home circle, where, at day's decline,
Her moulding power, her radiant virtues shine!
Not in the church to rule or teach, her place;
   Not in the mart of trade, or senate halls;
Not the wild, festive scene is hers to grace;
Not Fashion's altar her its victim calls;
Not here her field of triumph; but alone
She moves the queen of her own quiet home."

REV. MARK TRAFTON.

WOMAN A HELPMEET.

The purpose of God in the creation of woman was to provide man with a helpmeet. The language is unmistakable. "And the Lord God said, It is not good that the man should be alone. I will make for him a helper suited to him." Woman was made to be man's helpmeet in Eden; that purpose survives the *fall*. For right or wrong, for good or ill, her influence is felt. She lifts man up or drags him down. Scoff at it, oppose it, cast opprobrium upon this ancient utterance, the fact remains, woman is made for man.

Helpmeet she was, helpmeet she must be, or leave her work undone, and suffer the blight that results from the lack of love. God placed man in the garden to keep it, and he placed woman there to fill the bower with love, and his home with joy.

The coming of Eve to Adam is a beautiful story. He had been taught to realize his need of her. It was a part of his constitution. The same is true now wherever woman is appreciated. The felt want is the recognition of the fact. A wife chosen by one's parents, not by himself, is devoid of all of those special characteristics which distinguish her where processes of love begin, go on, deepen and tighten, until the bond is woven and the union formed.

"Nothing so delights man as those graceful nets,
Those thousand delicacies that daily flow
From all her words and actions, mixed with love
And sweet compliance, which declare unfeigned
Union of mind, or in them both one soul."[A]

[Footnote A: Paradise Lost, Book VIII.]

The knowledge of congeniality of tastes can only be obtained by mutual acquaintance, and by a careful study. It is said nothing is so blind as love. Nothing is so foolish as a blind love. Man needs a helpmeet, and woman needs a man she can help. It is possible to know before marriage that the parties are able to fulfil this trust. If they cannot fulfil it, marriage is a sin, which brings forth continuous sorrow and discontent.

The purpose of God to provide a helpmeet was avowed, but Adam did not know the fact. Under the arch of God's promise we discover the working of God's providence. The Bible, if properly studied, is a more thrilling narrative than any novel, because in it we can behold the infinite

God working with man and for man. "It is not good that man should be alone." This is the general proposition. As a counterpart we find man feeling that it was very sad to be alone. In his heart there is a want at work, making him ready for the blessing which God is preparing for him.

The want of the soul means a purpose on the part of God to supply it. This is true in regard to all that vitally interests man in this world. My want is the basis of my hope. God, who is above and around me, would not send forward the desire unless he had purposed to grant it.

Prayer stirring in the soul, is to man spiritually what a bill of goods preceding the payment is to a merchant. Do we long for salvation, for a revival, for any spiritual outpouring? have faith in God. There is a motive in it. Expect the blessing, and you will receive it.

"The Spirit itself," said Paul, "beareth witness with our spirit, that we are the children of God; and if children, then heirs; heirs of God, and joint heirs with Christ, if so be that we suffer with him, that we may be also glorified together." This is enjoyed despite the curse. "Jesus sent us the Comforter, who helpeth our infirmities, for we know not what we should pray for as we ought, but the Spirit itself maketh intercession for us with groanings which cannot be uttered. And he that searcheth the hearts knoweth what is the mind of the spirit, because he maketh intercession for the saints according to the will of God. And we know that all things work together for good to them that love God, to them who are thus called according to his purpose." This fatherhood of God comes to us under all circumstances and in all conditions. In the home, in the heart with all its wails, in the battle, in the victory, on earth and in heaven. Notice how Adam was made ready for his helpmeet.

"And out of the ground the Lord God formed every beast of the field, and every fowl of the air, and brought them unto Adam to see what he would call them; and whatsoever Adam called every living creature, that was the name thereof. And Adam gave names to all cattle, and to the fowl of the air, and to every beast of the field; but for Adam there was not found a helpmeet for him."

Imagine Adam feeling this want of companionship as the beasts of earth in their pristine beauty pass before him. There are those who mate with a horse or a dog. Who make a pet of a brute, and, ignoring their higher relations, live for their lower nature. We know that animals can be brought to do almost anything but talk, and some birds have the gift of speech. It was doubtless true of Eden. The serpent's talking did not surprise Eve.

Perhaps Adam may have found animals that could have kept him company. Yet he could find none who could meet his want as a helpmeet. Milton has fancifully described Adam expressing his want to the Infinite. It grew upon him. Then he has pictured him asleep, and seeing, as in a trance, the rib, with cordial spirits warm, formed and fashioned with his hands, until

"Under his forming hands a creature grew,
Manlike, but different sex, so lovely fair
That what seemed fair in all the world seemed now
Mean, or in her summed up, in her contained,
And in her looks, which from that time infused
Sweetness into my heart unfelt before,
And into all things from her air inspired
The spirit of love and amorous delight."

Then she disappeared. The dream haunted him in his waking hours. In the gallery of the Louvre there is a picture of Henry IV becoming entranced by the picture of his future wife, and next to it is the picture of the proud man being married to the woman whose face in the picture had once captivated his fancy. Those pictures were the realization of the one described in Milton's verse. Adam saw in Eve the realization of his dream, and was happy when he welcomed to his embrace this first gift of God, which met his want and answered his prayer. God created man not only a social being but an intellectual being. A beast can mate with beasts. They do so. A distinguished writer says, "the family relation is almost universal among the higher classes of animals." Adam's immortal nature longed for a kindred spirit. One to commune with, one to love, one to guide, one to look at life from another standpoint, one whose opinions should be diverse, and yet alike in difference, one to help in all the affairs of life, not only for the propagation of the species, but to provide things useful and comfortable for him, and like himself in temper, in disposition, and destiny. One to whom God shall be a loving Father, and heaven a common home. One with whom soul can join with soul in worship and love. A kindred spirit. A spirit having a common love, a common purpose, a common aspiration, and a common interest.

This longing for companionship was the earliest recorded emotion of the soul. It comes earliest to us and stays longest. In childhood, very often, instinct and desire rule wisely, and matches formed in heaven are recognized in life's morning on earth far oftener than we are accustomed to think. This longing never ceases. The child wants companionship, and old age, shattered and broken, feels the need of this loving support which God provides in the opposite sex quite as much as does the youthful heart. Our perfect humanity is made up of the two, and is not complete without this union.

The most magnificent scenery is tame, unless you can point out its beauties to the one you love. The picture gallery is worthless, unless some other lip can press the goblet of your pleasure, and sip nectar from the flower of beauty which blossoms in your thought or imagination. It is not good for man to be alone, even in Eden. Eden is not Eden without its Eve. Before Eve came, Eden was the pastureland of beasts; after it, the place took on home-like properties, bowers of love were formed, and the place became the house of God, and the gate of heaven.

The characteristics of woman as a helpmeet deserve our notice.

1. *Consider this word "Woman."* Woman was the name given to our mother because she was taken out of man. The word itself means *pliant*. In this definition we discover the first characteristic of a womanly nature. She is pliant. She adjusts herself to circumstances. She is adapted to meet man's wants, because she finds it in her nature to adapt herself to meet them.

It is gentlemanly to avow an opinion. We feel that it is womanly to waive one. We never think less of a woman for not forcing her opinions upon a company. We do not desire her to be without opinions, nor is it expected that she will desist from expressing an opinion, but if one must yield, it is womanly in woman to do so.

Indeed, oftentimes a woman of strong mental calibre, whose opinions are derived from thought and study, has built her husband up by permitting his expression to stand even though her own judgment might differ from him. If she be a true wife or sister, she will seek, in retirement, to correct an opinion which could not be avowed in public without weakening a husband's or a brother's influence. A woman that builds up another is herself a power and a praise.

The word *pliant* does not demand an absence of quality. The Damascus blade is pliant; it can be bent but it is not easily broken, while its edge is the keenest and its strength is a marvel. So woman is not necessarily weak because she is pliant. She may be the very reverse, and yet be pliant. Oftentimes her power of control is the more potent because it is unseen and unostentatious. An opinion held, to be uttered in the moment of cool and calm reflection, may be more telling than if spoken while the storm of debate was raging. The still, small voice came after the lightning and the thunder and the earthquake, and God spake in it with power and effect. It is the quiet utterance in the home which is of marvellous power in the world. It is womanly to adorn rather than to plan.

She fits herself for companionship rather than for leadership. By her tact and by her very nature she is enabled to harmonize antagonistic elements, and promote concord, if she cannot secure union. Like the lily living in the water, she feeds on her native element, love. The lily, though it floats on the wave, opens wider its leaves to the rain and dew. So woman, though living on love, finds pleasure and rapture in fresh manifestations of love day by day. It is her nature to love. It is her life to be beloved.

2. Think of this other title, *feminine*. This word, in its meaning, furnishes the second characteristic. It pertains to woman, and denotes a soft, tender, and delicate nature. Effeminate means destitute of manly qualities.

A woman truly feminine is thus described: "No coarseness was mingled with her plainness of speech; no boisterousness with her zeal. Her feelings, her sensibilities, her tastes were all characterized by a gentleness and delicacy seldom surpassed. While her heroic daring and unconquerable energy excited admiration, her love of birds and flowers, and indeed of all that is beautiful in nature, made her seem almost childlike." This characteristic, so loved and admired, is woman's glory, and yet it is effeminate. Woman's mind is quicker, more flexible, more elastic than man's, though the brain, in weight, is much lighter. Man's brain weighs, on an average, three pounds and eight ounces. Woman's brain weighs, on an average, two pounds and four ounces. The female intellect is impregnated with the qualities of her sensitive nature. It acts rather through a channel of electricity than of reasoning. Its perceptions of truth come, as it were, by intuition. It is under the influence of the heart, that has deep and unfathomable wells of feeling; and truth is felt in every pulse, rather than reasoned out and demonstrated. You cannot offend a woman so quick, in any way, as to ask her why she wishes to do thus, or why she reaches such a conclusion. Her reply is, invariably, "'*Cause!*" And that is about all she knows about it; and yet woe be to the man who ignores her intuitions, or treats with disdain her advice. Woman reads character quicker and better than man. Her policy lies in her heart. She feels rather than reasons. Man reasons rather than feels. Hence she is a helpmeet. She fills a lack, and supplies a want.

In her the imagination and fancy have such a lively play, that the homeliest principles assume forms of beauty. In intellectual pursuits she is destined to excel by her fine sensibilities, her nice observations, and exquisite tastes, while man is appointed to investigate the laws of abstruse sciences, and perform in literature and art the bolder flights of genius. She may surpass him in representing life and manners, and in the composition of letters, memoirs, and moral tales, in descriptive poetry, and in certain styles of music and painting, and even in sculpture. But she will never write an Iliad or a Paradise Lost, or tragedies like those of Aeschylus. She will never rival Demosthenes in producing a political oration, nor a massive philosophic history like Thucydides. She will not paint a Madonna like Raphael, nor chisel an Apollo Belvedere. The logic of Aristotle, the polemics of Augustine, the prodigious onsets of a Luther, the Institutes of a Calvin, the Novum Organum of Bacon, the Principia of Newton, the Cosmos of Humboldt—the like of these she will never achieve, nor is it desirable that she should.

Women seldom invent. There are all manner of inventions, often hundreds of applications in a single day, for patents at the Patent Office, yet among them there are no female applicants. Woman cannot compete with man in a long course of mental labor. The female mind is rather quiet and timid than fiery and driving. It admires rather than covets the great exploits of the other sex. Woman never excelled in architecture. To her belong the gentler arts of quiet life and retirement, where she has power to soften and refine the heart of him who is accustomed to battle with the elements and the forces of external nature.

We might speak at length of woman's gentle nature, present striking examples of female submission, endurance, and heroism, and speak in general of her charms and of her beneficent influence in domestic and social life. It would be equally pertinent, perhaps, to exhibit brilliant specimens of female genius and culture in the more graceful walks of literature, science, or art. These gay flowers of humanity lie scattered all over the vast field of history. But our subject leads us in another direction. Woman as a helpmeet finds in her own nature the natural introduction to the spheres of usefulness and influence ever open to her. She has a body, a mind, and soul. She must help, physically, mentally, and spiritually. The household partnership is opened to her physical nature. This relation is good as far at it goes. But it is only the beginning. It is rather the result than the commencement of the union. There is a closer tie found in intellectual companionship. Mind comes in contact with mind; the wants of the intellect are met, and a union is the result. Men engaged in public life, literary men and artists, have often found in their wives companions and confidantes in thought no less than in feeling. And as the intellectual development of woman has spread wider, and never higher, they have been mutual helpers, suited to each other. Roland and his wife in Paris, William and Mary Howitt of England, and Mr. and Mrs. Browning, are beautiful illustrations of this principle, though they are exceptional in their character. As a rule, when men find helpers in women, there is no community of employment. Harmony exists in difference no less than in likeness, if only the same key-note governs both parts. Woman the poem, man the poet! Woman the heart, man the head! Such instances lie all about us. Man rides to battle, while his wife is busy in the kitchen; but difference of occupation does not prevent that community of inward life, that perfect esteem which causes him to say, —

"Whom God loves, to him gives he such a wife"

And yet there is a still higher realm open before woman, because of her spiritual nature.

Woman as a helpmeet needs something besides a well-stored mind. She requires a heart filled with pure affections. Here we perceive how essential to her well being is submission to Christ.

The assumption of the New Testament is, that we possess an animal nature. The meaning of the word *flesh*, in all the New Testament writings, is, that the human family are living in an animal condition. It is taught that in that condition it is impossible for them to understand higher truths, or to feel higher influences, or to enter into the experiences which belong to the full development of the higher faculties. Christ came to us, suffered, and died for us, that an escape from this lower into the higher realm might be possible. It is possible. There is inherent under the divine influence the power of recreating, so that the soul shall escape from the prison-house of the flesh, and shall henceforth lead the mind and the body into a higher realm of thought and action. The very nature of woman makes her susceptible to religious impressions. Her lively imagination, her quick sensibilities, and her ready sympathy enable her readily to give Christ, the personification of every manly attribute and the embodiment of every virtue, a welcome to her soul.

It is possible for woman's spiritual nature to so marry Christ, that her physical nature can, without a great sacrifice, forego the joys of earthly companionship. Hence some women mated with a brute of a man, shine as Christians, and make excellent mothers. Woman as a Christian is a helpmeet indeed and in truth. Her power as such is felt in the church and in the world. She is peculiarly adapted to carry forward enterprises which have to do with meliorating the condition of society. Who is so adapted as she to manage an orphan's home, or to minister to the sick in hospitals, or to give support and sympathy to the aged, or to train children up in the nurture and admonition of the Lord? The first requisite to companionship is a heart imbued with the love of Christ. *A heart must be emphasized,* for a heartless woman is a terror in society, but a woman with a great heart, reverent and obedient to God, and full of love for Christ and his work, is a benefaction to a man, to a home, to a community, and to the world. "Favor is deceitful and beauty is vain, but a woman that feareth the Lord, she shall be praised." And a woman that feareth the Lord and serveth him, is praised and prized beyond rubies. The next requisite to holiness may be said to be skilfulness in the home. Woman must be trained to household duties. If she lacks here, she is wanting in much that makes her a real wife or mother or sister.

America, the land of homes, finds the housewife essential to its future. Housework in woman is ever honorable. It ought to be her glory and her pride. Let us make it so more and more.

The second requisite is intelligence. A woman must keep up with man in literature, in general news, in what interests the community, and especially in growth in grace, and in the knowledge of the word of God, if she would make her home attractive. Thus shall they

"Sit side by side full sunned in all their powers
Dispensing harvests;

Self-reverent each and reverencing each
Distinct in individualities;
But like each other even as those who love,
Then comes the statelier Eden back to man.
For it is possible in wedded pair a harmony
More grateful than harmonious sound to the ear."

Said Count Zinzendorf, in regard to his wife, "Twenty-five years' experience has shown me that just the helpmeet whom I love is the only one that could suit my vocation. Who else could have so carried through my family affairs? Who lived so spotlessly before the world? Who so wisely aided me in my rejection of a dry morality? Who so clearly set aside Pharisaism, which, as years passed, threatened to creep in among us? Who so deeply discerned as to the spirits of delusion which sought to bewilder us? Who would have governed my whole economy so wisely, richly, and hospitably, when circumstances commanded? Who have taken indifferently the part of servant or mistress without, on the one side, affecting an especial spirituality; on the other, being sullied by any worldly pride? Who, in a community where all ranks are eager to be on a level, would, from wise and real causes, have known how to maintain inward and outward distinctions? Who, without a murmur, has seen her husband encounter such dangers by land and sea? Who undertaken with him and sustained such astonishing pilgrimages? Who, amid such difficulties, would have always held *up her head and supported me*? Who found such vast sums of money and acquitted them on her own credit? And, finally, who, of all human beings, could so well understand and interpret to others my inner and outer being, as this one, of such nobleness in her way of thinking, such great intellectual capacity, and so free from the theological perplexities that enveloped me?" Let any one peruse, with all intentness, the lineaments of this portrait, and he will be impressed with the fact, that it is possible for woman to fulfil her mission, and become a true helpmeet. This woman was not a copy. She was not a cipher. She was an original; and while she loved and honored her husband, she thought for herself on all subjects, with so much intelligence, that he could and did look on her as a sister and friend also.

The third and highest grade of marriage union is the religious, which may be expressed "as a pilgrimage round a common shrine." This includes the other,—home sympathies and household wisdom,—for these pilgrims know how to assist each other along the dusty way.

These facts should be remembered in her education. The beautiful forms which everywhere exist in nature should be impressed upon the female mind, and the treasures of elegant literature should be opened to her in no stinted measure.

A well-disciplined and a well-stored mind she does indeed require; but a heart of pure affections, a lively imagination, and quick sensibilities to give depth, and form, and beauty, and vivacity to the character of her mind, are so peculiarly feminine accomplishments, that without them a woman of the greatest intellect is, as it were, unsexed and disrobed of her loveliest charms. She may be a Queen Elizabeth, and conquer a Spanish Armada, but she will never conquer the heart, nor be recognized as a model of female character. She is to be the mother of her race. This fixes the sphere of her duties in the home. Think of Helen Olcott, the wife of Rums Choate; of the first Mrs. Webster, and of her influence upon that man who won the proud appellation, "The Great Expounder."

The story is told of Daniel Webster meeting a woman with her two boys loaded down with bundles, at the Jersey Ferry, in New York. The lady had lost her fortune through the failure of her husband. She was poor, and the old set ignored her. But she lived in a little cottage in New Jersey, and made it bright with her face of love. She was tired and sad. Many had passed her. Mr. Webster, seeing her perplexity, offered to relieve her of her bundles, and take charge of one of the boys. They entered the cars. He talked to her of her God-given trust, of her work, and of the results that would naturally flow from her efforts; of the province of a mother, of the trust reposed in her by God himself. She was encouraged and strengthened, and when she came to the depot, she said, "Please, sir, give me your card, that I may mention your name to my husband." She hurried out, and looked at it, and saw the name of Daniel Webster. The woman was thrilled with the joy that came to her in her sphere of service. Earth knows no fairer, holier relation than that of mother; and she turned with delight from the bubbles and froth of fashion to the grand work before her of raising men for God and humanity.

"The treasures of the deep are not so precious
As are the concealed comforts of a man
Locked up in woman's love. I scent the air
Of blessings when I come but near the house.
What a delicious breath marriage sends forth!
The violet bed's not sweeter."

Think of the realm in which woman may rule. If she be elegant and refined; if she has learned how to govern, first herself, and then those about her, there is a charm diffused through the home which reveals itself in the good order of the establishment, in the politeness of the servants, in the genial disposition of the children, in the delightful intercourse of the different portions of the household, and in the fact that "her husband is known in the gates when he sitteth among the elders of the land. Strength and honor are her clothing, and she shall rejoice in time to come. She openeth her mouth with wisdom, and her tongue is the law of kindness. She looketh well to the ways of her household, and eateth not the bread of idleness. Her children rise up and call her blessed; her husband also, and he praiseth her. Many daughters have done virtuously; but thou excellest them all."

In such words did King Lemuel praise this excellency of woman. Blessed memory! Who does not remember that one form of the old-fashioned mother,—the law of whose life was love; one who was the divinity of our infancy, and the sacred presence in the shrine of our first earthly idolatry; one whose heart was ever green, though the snows of time had gathered in the boughs of her life-tree; one to whom we never grow old, but in the plumed troop or the grave council are children still; one who welcomed us coming, blessed us going, and forgets us never; one who waits for the echo of our returning footstep, or who, perhaps, has gone on to the better land, and keeps a light in the window for those left behind.

Such women have power now as did the Hannahs and the Ruths of the olden time. When thinking of them, you are convinced that, young or old, they remain among the best of God's gifts to man. This leads us to remark further, that woman's right to be a woman implies her right to help woman. Woman must be true to her sex, or society will neglect its duty. That old story of Ruth and Naomi has ploughed through the world, because it reveals woman's power as a helper. Ruth clung to Naomi, and Naomi helped her daughter to find Boaz, that noble prince in Israel; and so she became identified with the succession of promise. The life of Mrs. Sigourney illustrates the same truth. See her among the young, calling forth their powers, and starting them in a career of usefulness. Impressed with the importance of an education, she aided by her pen, as by her example, to induce the ladies of her acquaintance to obtain a thorough knowledge of the primary branches that enter into daily use.

We want a woman to be intellectual without being puny. We ask that she remain a pliant vine, and that she be not made into the rugged oak.

Woman owes it to herself that she be fitted to occupy any position in society. In this land, as in no other, the barriers of caste are removed, and every line of separation obliterated. The rich and the poor meet together.

The cultured sewing-girl is quite likely to become the wife of the future millionnaire; and the lady reared in the midst of every luxury, and endowed with a fortune, amid the reverses of fortune may be compelled to draw upon her own resources of labor, and of love, and culture, to stay up the hands and encourage the heart of the man more than ever dependent upon her for happiness and hope.

Such a woman Irving must have painted when he wrote, "I have often had occasion to remark the fortitude with which women sustain the most overwhelming reverses of fortune. Those disasters which break down the spirit of a man, and prostrate him in the dust, seem to call forth all the energies of the softer sex, and give such intrepidity and devotion to their character, that at times it approaches to sublimity."

Nothing can be more touching than to behold a soft and tender female, who had been all weakness, and dependence, and alive to every trivial roughness, while treading the prosperous paths of life, suddenly rising in mental force to be the comforter and supporter of her husband under misfortunes, and abiding, with unshrinking firmness, the bitterest blasts of adversity.

As the vine, which has long twined its graceful foliage about the oak, and been lifted by it into sunshine, will, when the lordly plant is rifted by the thunderbolt, cling round it with caressing tendrils, and bind up its shattered boughs, so it is beautifully ordained by Providence that woman, who is the mere dependent and ornament of man in his happier hours, should be his stay and solace when smitten with sudden calamity; winding herself into the rugged recesses of his nature, tenderly supporting the head and binding up the broken heart.

To fill this feature of the wife, education is essential in household affairs, quite as much as education in books, in music, and the ways of fashion is essential to the young wife whose husband has suddenly become rich, and has given up his chambers and taken an elegant house in some fashionable street.

It is as bad to fall from the heights of opulence, and know not how to sweep a room, make a bed, or cook a meal, as it is to rise to an exalted position, and know not how to welcome company or preside at a feast.

The women in America who suddenly become elevated in rank, and buy pictures by the yard and books by the cord, are quite as abundant as are those who lose fortune and rank, and are compelled to seek menial employments.

The happiness secured by the proper employment of time, and by the cultivation of the mind, furnishes a high incentive to exertion.

Contrast the woman who is educated with the one uneducated. See her in her home, reigning a queen, while her uneducated sister, though she may have wealth and beauty, will constantly feel the lack of that which gold cannot procure nor fortune provide. "We are foolish, and without excuse foolish," said Ruskin, "in speaking of the 'superiority' of one sex to the other, as if they could be compared in similar things. Each has what the other has not; each completes the other, and is completed by the other; they are in nothing alike; and the happiness and perfection of both depend on each asking and receiving from the other what the other only can give.

WOMAN AS A TEMPTER.

It will be admitted by all who will read the history of man's ruin, as recorded in Genesis, the third chapter, and sixth verse, that woman first partook of the forbidden fruit, and "gave also to her husband, and he did eat." Admit the truth of history, and woman appears as man's first tempter.

"Woman as a Helpmeet" described her condition before the fall; "Woman as a Tempter" describes her in the fall; and, alas! while it is the high privilege of woman to be a helpmeet in the midst of the ruin wrought by sin, it is unwise to disguise the truth that as a *tempter* she has not abandoned her vocation.

Plain speaking may prove to be disagreeable. God grant that it may prove to be profitable. There is need of it. Disguise it as we may talk as we choose about man in his narrowness, in his degradation, a wicked woman *was*, and to a large extent *is*, the means employed by Satan in leading astray the unwary. The manner of her fall has been declared. It may be profitable to review the steps of her downward descent from the bliss of Eden to the woe of the desert; from the position of an equal to the position of a subject.

1. *Satan, in the form of the serpent, undermines woman's confidence in God.* The serpent, the most subtle beast of the field, said to the woman, "Is it even so, that God has said, Ye shall not eat of every tree of the garden?" Thus he attempted to weaken the child-like confidence she reposed in her

Creator, and endeavored to inspire in its place a spirit of unbelief and distrust. This done, and the battle was half won, and the work was well nigh accomplished. Truly has it been said, "The sure basis of simple trust in God as the all-loving and the all-wise, once shaken, there is little left to be done." This is the rock on which character builds its hopes. There is nothing so essential to woman as faith in God. Destroy this, or let woman attempt to live without it, and she is in imminent peril. It was an infidel woman who declared, "It has been said that marriage is a divine institution, because all power comes from God. *We know very well that all power comes from God', and therefore we wish neither God nor power.*" Shall professedly Christian women, by action, give their assent to such an utterance?

2. *Satan rouses woman's suspicion.* "And the woman said to the serpent. Of the fruit of the trees of the garden we may eat. But of the fruit of the tree which is in the midst of the garden God has said, Ye shall not eat of it, and ye shall not touch it, lest ye die. And the serpent said to the woman, Ye shall not surely die. For God knows that in the day ye eat thereof your eyes will be opened, and ye will be as God, knowing good and evil."

"Your eyes will be opened," expresses the power of mentally apprehending things before unperceived and unknown; but, of course, both in an intellectual and moral sense. The position taken appeared reasonable, and had a semblance of truth, and exerted its consequent influence.

"*Will be as God, knowing good and evil.*" Knowing for yourselves, and able to choose between the evil and the good. Here ambition again overleaped itself. Humility was slain, and a womanly virtue was destroyed by the tempter, who aimed to infuse into the mind of the woman, first, a doubt of the truth of the Word of God, and of the certainty of the divine threatening; second, a suspicion that God was withholding from her a good, instead of guarding her against an evil; and, third, he attempted to induce her to believe that adherence to this divine command stood in the way of her freedom, of her growth, and so by the words, "Ye will be as God, knowing good and evil," he strove to awaken the feeling of self-exaltation,—the longing for a higher development, in which she should attain to self-discretion and freedom of choice and action.

This suspicion is very common, even among our good women. When a woman gets cold in her love for Jesus, she becomes suspicious of those she loves. She permits the feeling, "My husband gives too much for benevolence, too little to me, and he is away too much in meetings, and is too little in his home," to influence her. She begins to talk against the church, and loves to stay at home. Finds excuses for keeping away from the prayer meeting or from the paths of endeavor, and becomes a hinderance instead of a blessing to husband, to family, and to society. A man finds it difficult to push the bark of benevolence and of holy endeavor up against the current of womanly opposition and suspicion, but when in the work of God she acts the part of a helpmeet, everything moves smoothly. A recent writer uses this language: "Expel woman as you will, she is in fact the parish. Within, in her lowest spiritual form, as the ruling spirit she inspires, and sometimes writes the sermons. Without, as the bulk of his congregation, she watches over his orthodoxy, verifies his texts, visits his schools, and harasses his sick." ... "The preacher who thunders so defiantly against spiritual foes, is trembling all the time beneath the critical eye that is watching him with so merciless an accuracy in his texts. Impelled, guided, censured by woman, we can hardly wonder if, in nine cases out of ten, the parson turns woman himself, and the usurpation of woman's rights in the services of religion has been deftly avenged by the subjugation of the usurpers. Expelled from the temple, woman has simply put her priesthood into commission, and discharges her ministerial duties by proxy." Woman is the mainspring and the chief support of Ritualism. Things were at a dead lock and stand still, until the so-called devotion gave an impetus to the movement. The medieval church have glorified the devotion of woman; but once become a devotee, it had locked her in the cloister. As far as action in the world without was concerned, the veil served simply as a species of suicide, and the impulses of woman, after all the crowns and pretty speeches of her religious counsellors, found themselves bottled up within stout stone walls, and as inactive as before. From this strait woman released herself by the organization of charity. The Sisters of Charity at once became a power. They discovered the value of costume. The district visitor, whom nobody had paid the smallest attention to in the common vestments of the world, became a sacred being as she donned the crape and hideous bonnet of the "Sister."

"The 'Mother Superior' took the place of the tyrant of another sex who had hitherto claimed the submission of woman; but she was something more to her 'children' than the husband or father whom they had left in the world without. In all matters, ecclesiastical as well as civil, she claimed within her dominions to be supreme. The quasi-sacerdotal dignity, the pure religious ministration which ages have stolen from her, was quietly resumed. She received confessions, she imposed penances, she drew up offices of devotion. If the clergyman of the parish ventured an advice or suggestion, he was told that the sisterhood must preserve its own independence of action, and was snubbed home again for his pains. The Mother Superior, in fact, soon towered into a greatness far beyond the reach of ordinary persons. She kept her own tame chaplain, and she kept him in a very edifying subjugation. From a realm completely her own, the influence of woman began to tell upon the world without. Little colonies of Sisters, planted here and there, annexed parish after parish. Astonished congregations saw their church blossom its purple and red, and frontal and hanging told of the silent energy of the group of Sisters. The parson found himself nowhere, in his own parish: every detail managed for him, every care removed, and all independence gone. If it suited the ministering angels to make a legal splash, he found himself landed in the law courts. If they took it into their heads to seek another field, every one assumed it a matter of course that their pastor would go too." It is because of this influence that in certain quarters the ecclesiastical hierarchy are taking, year by year, a more feminine position. It is not impossible that a church who worships Mary as the Mother of God may be brought to recognize woman as the proper head of the church. True, as the writer quoted above adds, "she must stoop to conquer heights like these." Yet the question has been seriously asked, "Is not the Episcopal office admirably adapted to woman?" Between a priest and a nun there is only the difference of a bonnet in their dress, and we know how easily woman can be persuaded to go without a bonnet, or to exchange it for a hat such as is worn by men. In England, the curate is sometimes called the first lady of the parish; and what he now is in theory, a century hence may find him in fact. "It would be difficult, even now, to detect any difference of sex in the triviality of purpose, the love of gossip, the petty interests, the feeble talk, the ignorance, the vanity, the love of personal display, the white hand dangled over the pulpit, the becoming vestment, and the embroidered stole, which we are learning gradually to look upon as attributes of the British curate. So perfect, indeed, is the imitation, that the excellence of her work may, perhaps, defeat its own purpose, and the lacquered imitation of woman may satisfy the world, and for long ages prevent any anxious inquiry after the real feminine Brummagem."

The tendency thus truthfully described furnished the seedling out of which grew the Monasticism of the past, and in which the Ritualism of the present finds its underlying cause. The Church of Rome harnesses woman to her system, and compels her to contribute greatly to its prosperity. In Europe the people tire of those great establishments and endowments, which rest like an incubus on the national life. In America we are so blind that we foster them by grants from our legislatures, by giving up the care of hospitals to their use, where the weak are subjected to the influences of superstition, and the thoughtless are led astray. Another avenue to power is opened by the ballot. Grant this to that church, which, through a fatherhood of priests and a sisterhood of nuns, reaches every portion of the body politic, and the promise of Religious Liberty and a Free Republic is at once exchanged for the despotism of Rome and the imperialism of France. Infidelity joins hands with Rome in asking this power. Christianity, united with patriotism, must refuse to grant the request.

3. Mystery was employed as an instrument in securing woman's fall. Rouse a womanly curiosity, and there is little difficulty in leading the excited one astray. Hold out to her a key which promises to unlock the hidden and concealed glories of the unexplored future, and woman will be tempted again to forego God's favor and the joys of paradise to grasp or wield it. In every heathen religion women occupied a prominent place. Priestess or prophetess, she stood in all ministerial offices on an equality with man. Christianity rejects the ministerial services of women, and selects for its standard bearers men acquainted with life, filled with religious zeal, and capable of hardy endeavor, assuring faith and martyr patience.

The Church of Rome dealt with women as the Empire dealt with its Caesars: it was ready to grant her apotheosis, but only when she was safely out of this world. It was only when the light of revelation was extinguished in her midst that the teachings of the Bible were ignored, and woman was welcomed back to the place she held in pagan climes and at heathen shrines.

Spiritualism, that scourge of modern times, which has swept like the breath of a pestilence over the land, found in woman its prophetess and minister. Satan works in erring woman now, as in the past, to destroy and to delude. That power was resisted by Christian woman. Many an irreligious man was saved from this delusion by the fidelity of his wife. Many a good man has been ruined because his wife listened to the siren voice of the tempter, and desired to explore and explain this mystery. The forbidden fruit ever grows upon the tree beside her. Those who would be wiser than that which is written, have plucked and eaten it, and have given to others that which is so destructive. Witchcraft is a womanly profession. The heathen divinities were nearly all ministered unto by woman, and mystery was the influencing cause. We know the result in the case of Eve. It led her away from God. It caused her to listen to the enemy of her soul. Does it not become woman to ask herself, "Am I losing my hold on God? Is suspicion that some good is being withheld, or does the desire to pry into the future, exercise an undue influence upon my heart and imagination?" If so, your ruin has commenced, and a speedy return to God is your only door of escape.

4. Deception was the result. "And the woman saw the tree was good for food, and that it was a delight to the eyes, and that the tree was to be desired to make her wise; and she took of its fruit and ate, and gave also to her husband and he ate." Sight deceived, desire allured, and action born of a delusive faith destroyed her happiness. The process of temptation culminated in deception. This is the end ever kept in view by Satan. Every individual that refuses to be ruled absolutely by God, in little or great affairs, may know of a truth that the end is deception, and the consequent ruin is sure to follow. There is no exception to the rule. Paul felt this when he wrote the church in Corinth, concerning his interest in them, saying, "For I am jealous over you with a godly jealousy; for I have espoused you to one husband, that I may present you as a chaste virgin to Christ;" "But I fear, lest by any means, as the serpent beguiled Eve, by his subtlety, so your minds should be corrupted from your simplicity toward Christ." Many claim that error is not mischievous while truth is left free to combat. Error

poisons the mind, and so produces disease, and bars out truth, which carries health to the mind and blesses the soul.

Eve knew the law, for she quotes it word by word. She deliberated as to obeying it. Here she made her first mistake. A woman cannot do this. The moment a woman hesitates in regard to discharging the duties she owes to herself or to God she falls. She seems to be provided with an almost self-acting nature. It is natural for her to protect herself. She revolts against her higher self when she hesitates. Her intuitions, allied to a sensitive nature, unite in defending against evil. Had Eve said, "I do not need to sin to secure the development of my higher nature; the Creator knows my wants much better than one who seeks to be my destroyer," she would have been saved. Faith in God would have been a sure defence against the tempter's wiles.

But she deliberated, yielded, and fell, and the world is still full of the resounding echoes of that fall. The race fell with her. That fact teaches its lesson. Some one falls with every ruined soul. We lift up or drag down those associated with us. "For none of us liveth to himself, and no man dieth to himself;" an influence goes out from us, which is a felt power in the world either for or against God and humanity.

Consider the effects of the temptation. 1. It caused Eve to become to Adam an agent of Satan. Tempted herself, she became a tempter. Ruined in her nature by this exclusion of God, and by this welcome of Satan, she seeks to ruin her companion. This principle rules now. The carnal heart is at enmity with God, the converted heart is in union with God. Here is a significant fact. A man loves to have woman pure, if he is impure. Temperate, if he is intemperate. Holy and Christian, if he is the opposite in every particular. Not so a woman. Intemperate herself, she seeks to induce others to be like her. Here is the peril of society. If our fashionable women love wine, they become emissaries of the wicked one to a fearful extent. It is almost an impossibility for the tempted to withstand their wiles. In fashionable, perhaps, more than in the other grades of life, woman as a leader in intemperance, in extravagance, and in opposition to Christ, is to be feared. Her power is fearful to contemplate. The Secretary of the Treasury declares that the national debt is increased, and threatens to increase, unless the fashionable world shall declare against the, importation of that which costs gold, but which fails to contribute to the prosperity of the community. This is by no means wholly chargeable to women. Men share in the blame. A sadder fact is the expressed dissatisfaction with woman's work and with woman's sphere. The home of the olden time is passing out of mind, and in its place is the fashionable boarding-house. The skilled housewife is felt to be unappreciated. Men, they tell us, prefer a pretty face to a noble heart, a delicate to a skilled hand, a girl who can play the piano rather than one who can cook a dinner, a pretty doll instead of a glorious woman capable of keeping the house, and of guiding the man with womanly strength. Ah, it is a mistake. America is the land of homes. Our undeveloped territory offers to every man a farm. Men and women need not to be cooped up in garrets or shut up in cellars, if they will but possess the spirit of those who sought in this Western world a home, and who, as they toiled with the axe, the plough, and the loom,

"Shook the depths of the forest gloom
With their hymns of lofty cheer."

The cause of this discontent is apparent. There is something in the commonplaces of fashionable life which turns woman from the real to the unreal, from the substantial to the superficial, which smothers all originality of thought, and makes her a simple reproduction in appearance, if not in disposition, of the "Anonyma," with her meretricious beauty and dashing toilets. Is it well for woman to subject herself to be criticised as follows? "The girl of the period is a creature who dyes her hair and paints her face, whose sole idea of life is a plenty of fun and luxury, and whose dress is the object of such thought and intellect as she possesses. Her main endeavor is to outvie her neighbors. She cares little for advice or counsel. Nothing is too extraordinary, and nothing too extravagant, for her vitiated taste; and things which in themselves would be useful reforms if let alone, become monstrosities worse than those which they have displaced, so soon as she begins to manipulate and improve. If a sensible fashion lifts the gown out of the mud, she raises hers midway to the knee. If there is a reaction against an excess of hair oil, and hair slimy and sticky with grease is thought less nice than if left clean with a healthy crisp, she dries and frizzes and sticks hers out on end like certain savages in Africa, or lets it wander down her back like Madge Wildfire's, and thinks herself all the more beautiful the nearer she approaches in look to a maniac or a negress! What the *demi-monde* does in its frantic efforts to excite attention, she also does in imitation. If some fashionable courtesan is reported to have come out with her dress below her shoulder blades, and a gold strap for all the sleeve thought necessary, the girl of the period follows suit next day, and then wonders that men sometimes mistake her for her prototype, or that mothers of girls, not so far gone as herself, refuse her as a companion for their daughters."

If the fashionable danseuse is imported from the brothels of Paris, and is brought to our cities to exhibit herself to whoever is vulgar and lewd enough to desire to see her, thousands of the fashionables go with opera glass, and tolerate a disgusting play that they may enjoy a sight which is a guarantee to every young man that the woman knows little of and cares less about the virtue which distinguished the girl of the olden time, before whom men bowed in admiration, and concerning whom an impure thought seemed like an unpardonable sin. Women may say that "men desire them to go, and they must gratify them." It is not true. Every man loves to have his wife and daughters virtuous, and unless he be besotted by intemperance, or given over to courses of shame, will quietly and joyfully yield to the remonstrance of a virtuous wife or daughter against patronizing scenes which degrade, and against permitting the mind and heart to give welcome to thoughts which pollute. True men desire to love, and to be influenced by pure, tender, loving, retiring, and domestic women.

Woman, it is your fault if you do not retain the affections of a true and noble man. Alas, how frequently young men mourn your fickleness, your frivolity, your fondness for show and dress, and your total lack of desire for the more solid attainments which enrich character, and beautify life. "Who can find a virtuous woman? for her price is far above rubies." Whoever conforms to the requirements of fashion, at the expense of culture, is false to her high nature, and degrades herself in the estimation of every true man. A woman is constructed for companionship, and in her normal condition her yearnings are more mental than physical. It is natural for man to desire to enjoy this God-given boon. A talented woman, that will talk sense, is the idol of sensible men. Nothing displeases a true woman more than to waste an evening on a brainless fop. Nothing is more needless. Let her develop herself, and she will be sought after by men whose opinions are valuable, and whose love is a recompense. Better far would it be for women who are poor, to spend their evenings in reading, writing, and study, in familiarizing themselves with those themes of ennobling thought, which will fit them to win love by conversation, by culture, by the graces of refinement, rather than by the outward adorning, by plaiting the hair, and wearing of gold and of costly apparel; "for it is the hidden man of the heart, even the ornament of a meek and quiet spirit, which is in the sight of God of great price."

Young women need to be reminded of this. They are in peril. Exposure lines the paths of those who pass from the factory, or from the workshop, to their little rooms and cheap boarding-houses. You see it in the leering look of depraved men, and in the atmosphere of crime that contaminates their shops. They show it by their themes of conversation. Woman must be resolute, if she would change all this. Let her be true to herself and to Christ, and there will be no danger. The condition of women in many of our factory villages is frightful to contemplate, and few seem to have any knowledge of it. They pass from their factory to their boarding-houses. Their rooms are cold and cheerless in winter. There is no common reading-room or sewing-room. Unless they will suffer from cold, they must retire to their beds, or seek warmth and companionship in the world without. As a result they are watched by men who care not for their comfort or happiness, but for the gratification of passion and the pleasures of social excitements. Hence, thousands of good country girls are annually ruined in many of our large factory villages and cities, for the lack of comfortable houses or associations, where talents can be cultivated, piety promoted, and virtue protected.

1. "*She gave to her husband, and he did eat.*" It was altogether natural. She was the provider in the home, as he was the keeper of the garden. She gave him and he ate. Man fell because of woman's fall. A woman can repel a man. It is difficult for a man to resist the wiles of a woman. God has placed in woman a fearful power, and devolves unmeasured responsibilities upon her in the home, in society, and in the world.

2. The second result is seen in the effect produced. "Lust conceived and brought forth sin, and sin brought forth shame." And the eyes of both of them were opened, not so as to have an advanced knowledge of things pleasant, profitable, and useful, as was promised and expected, but of things very disagreeable and distressing. Their eyes were opened to see that they had broken God's law, lost his favor, destroyed their home, and left themselves exposed to the terrors of the judgment. They heard the voice of the Lord God walking in the garden in the cool of the day, and Adam and his wife hid themselves from the presence of the Lord God among the trees of the garden.

They knew that they were naked. In place of conscious innocence and purity came the sense of guilt and shame. "We are not to understand," says Dr. Conant, "that there is allusion here to any physical effect of the eating of the forbidden fruit. So gross a conception is foreign to the spirit and purpose of the narrative. As the language in ch. ii. v. 5, is an expression of purity and peace of mind, so the language used here is the expression of conscious guilt, of self-condemnation and shame." Look at that criminal arrested. See him shiver as if cold. His nature is exposed because it is weakened. Righteousness is a defence. A man in sweet communion with God is girded with strength and endurance, with recuperative energies, of which a man is ignorant when he is alienated from God, and exposed to wrath. "For the word of God is living and powerful, and sharper than any two-edged sword, piercing even to the dividing asunder of soul and spirit, of joints and marrow, and is a discerner of the thoughts and intents of the heart. And there is no creature that is not manifest in his sight; but all things are naked and opened to the eyes of Him with whom we have to do." The Lord God was abroad. They hid themselves. They were afraid. Ah, there is a nakedness which the culprit feels, which cannot be covered up. God's eye pierces through every form of concealment, and lays bare the cause of ruin and the deed of shame. It is impossible to hide from God. If this world is deceived by our disguises, and pasteboard faces, and long robes, the Being with whom we have to do shall laugh at our calamities and mock when our fear cometh, as we shall stand out in our true characters, and shall be judged for the deeds done in the body, whether they be good or evil.

3. Sin not only changed their relations to each other, awakening their animal nature and killing their spiritual hope of sweet communion with God, but it changed their relations towards God. They became aliens to him. They lost their love, and were tortured by fear. They feared him whom they once loved. "And Jehovah God called to the man, and said to him, Where art thou? And he said, I heard thy voice in the garden, and was afraid

because I was naked, and hid myself. And he said, Who has showed thee that thou art naked? Hast thou eaten of the tree which I commanded thee not to eat? And the man said, The woman whom thou gavest to be with me, she gave me of the tree, and I ate."

Adam, in his beginnings of sin, furnishes an example to sinners, which has been abundantly copied. He says, "The woman whom thou gavest to be with me, she gave me of the tree, and I ate." He finds fault with God the giver, and fails to condemn woman the sinner. The passage is sometimes falsely interpreted, as an unworthy attempt of the man to cast the blame of his offence on the woman. But the emphasis lies on the words *whom thou gavest to be with me,* by which utterance he seeks to transfer the responsibility from himself to God, who gave him the companion by whose example he was betrayed into sin, instead of placing it upon the woman, who was the guilty cause. Thus he refuses or neglects to denounce the sin; but takes for granted that woman was as God made her, and acted in accordance with her mechanism. Hence, Adam argued, if any one was responsible, it was her Maker. She acted in accordance with the nature which had been given her. We hear this doctrine advanced daily. "I am what God made me." A cotton mill weaves cotton because it was made to weave cotton. It is not responsible. It weaves well or ill in accordance with the skill of the mechanism, and not in accordance with the desire of the proprietor. If it weaves ill, you blame the maker. If well, you praise the maker. Adam, in his reply, ignored woman's moral nature, and talked of her as though she had been a machine. "The woman whom thou gavest to be with me, she gave me of the tree, and I ate." He forgot his own higher nature, forgot his position, and fell. How he differed from the second Adam we shall see before we are done.

It is noticeable, not only that Adam ignored woman's moral nature, and the ruin wrought by sin, but he asserts a truth. Woman was given to man to provide him with food, to spread the feast, and to keep the house; and in her vocation, and while performing the duties assigned her, she led him astray. It is noteworthy that God does not reply to Adam, but turns to woman with the question, "*What is this that thou hast done?*" recognizing the fact that she turned from God, and turned towards God's enemy, and in listening, sinned; and in sinning, fell; and in falling, carried with her man; and in carrying man, whelmed the race in the ruin of the fall.

In speaking of woman as a tempter, we are not to forget that she is woman. The serpent beguiled her, and she ate. Satan found in her an ally; an so pleased was he with the results of the partnership he has never dissolved the firm. While woman, as a helpmeet, becomes an ally of Christ, as a tempter she is the ally of Satan. Not as a woman, but as a tempter, she is the ally of the evil one. Satan works in her, as a tempter, both to will and to do according to his good pleasure, whenever she submits to his sway. The reason for this is recorded in the Word of God. Some sneer at the reference to this time-honored record; but we reassert the truth. The Bible is the revealed will of God, and it declares the God-given sphere of woman. The Bible is, then, our authority for saying woman must content herself with this sphere, and try to meet its responsibilities, or she will lose self-respect and cast away the regard of the community. Without the Bible, her life is everywhere proven to be gloomy. With it, and beneath its protection, she becomes an heir of hope.

Notice the characteristics of her power as a tempter.

1. She is regarded as God's best gift to man. She fills a place in man's heart which is empty without her. It is difficult to think of her as an ally of Satan. We prefer to think of her as God's first and best gift to man. Even a fallen woman is regarded as a poor unfortunate, and is tolerated because the many claim she has been more sinned against than sinning. Excuses are

woven for her, out of the statements ever afloat, that she was in a starving condition, and was driven to desperation; that she was turned out upon the world, was deceived, led astray, and shipwrecked, and then did not care, and so went from bad to worse, until she became the wreck of her former self, and was given up to lust and the pollutions of shame. God forbid that we should cast stones at her. In the words of Christ, let us rather say to every fallen woman, "Go, *and sin no more*." But when a woman persists in sinning, we should speak of her in the language of Scripture, and boldly warn against her wiles.

A fallen woman is not God's gift to man. Before her fall she was God's gift. In beauty Eve still remains the model. The artist delights to paint her, and the poet sings her praises. But in conduct she is a warning. Scripture pictures her going to Adam, hiding from him the ruin wrought, and pressing to his lips the fruit which carried death. (Then she was the devil's gift to a sin-cursed world.) A fallen woman—a woman who refuses to love Christ and to serve him, who sweeps out into the paths of dissipation and of lust, and becomes a seductive wile—is the devil's ally; "for she forsaketh the guide of her youth, and forgetteth the covenant of her God. For her house inclineth unto death. None that go unto her returneth again, neither take they hold of the paths of life."

Against such a woman God warns us in the thunder tones of wrath, and the picture of her doom is lurid with the glow of the devouring flames, "for her feet go down to death and her steps take hold on hell."

This is but a single characteristic of her power as a tempter, and we love to think that it is the least employed. A mind retaining the perception of woman's worth, shrinks from the idea of linking her name with impurity. We cherish the hope that she is virtuously inclined, and cannot bear to think that she willingly forsakes the right and casts herself down the steeps of ruin. Ah, woman, when this is not the case society has a right to cast you off. It is because of this faith that the good despise the woman who persists in folly, and who secretly tries to seduce the unwary. God's judgments seem not too severe, and the language is none too strong, though the denunciation is terrible and the destruction certain. God makes no apologies for sin. A fallen woman is an abomination. Her crimes are terrible. She is the foe of the home, and the enemy of all that is pure. Hence she is thrown out upon the rocks, and left there to die, unpitied and unbefriended, without God and without hope in the world. By every virtuous person she is despised. Hence, between a virtuous woman and ruin there is a bridged chasm; whoever crosses that bridge leaves hope, and honor, and happiness behind. Think of the thousands about us going, unprayed for, down to perdition!

Society tolerates a man as it does not tolerate a woman. God did business with Adam, but he does not mention Eve after her fall. Society recognizes a fallen man as it cannot recognize a fallen woman. Thus her crime is proclaimed to be the greater than man's, even by the world. Let us be just. We do not heap the blame all on woman, even of her fall. All we say is, she bears the burden of the woe. In this fact she is warned. Society may pity her: it cannot palliate her guilt. Thus is she advised against throwing herself away, and casting off her allegiance to Christ, to herself, and to humanity. Let her fall, and almost without exception she is hopelessly ruined. Society points the finger of scorn at her, and, what is worse, the barriers to virtue having been broken down, they seem to be destroyed. It is as difficult to get back what a woman loses when she falls, as it would have been to have forced an entrance back into Eden after the banishment.

2. The fact that she is a woman gives her influence. In her terrible work beauty is an aid. God says, "Desire not her beauty in thy heart, neither let her take thee with her eyelids." That is, look for something besides a pretty face or a twinkling eye. "Pretty is that pretty does," is a good motto, and

utters a truth which is quite too frequently ignored. Beauty is not to be despised or condemned. God, who painted the lilies' bloom, and covered the sky with the wondrous tints of a glowing sunset, must enjoy beauty, and surely made it to please and to bless us. Yet when it comes to be used as an agent of evil, it is to be shunned and disregarded. In all this world there is nothing so empty as a heartless, brainless woman, with a pretty face. Yet beauty is a power; so the heathen declare, "Every woman would rather be handsome than good." That may be true in heathen, but it is not true of all in Christian climes. If there is one woman who thinks more of dress than duty, more of shadow than substance, more of Vanity Fair than of Virtue's bower, then beware. You are not an ally of Christ. At once begin a new life, if you would shun the dangers and avoid the terrible doom threatening you. Cast away that which excites passions and gives the body unrest, and seek the food for mind and soul which gives rest and peace. Seek Christ, and through him victory over self and over sin. Do something to brighten your home life and to honor your Master. Clear your soul from the taint of vanity. Do not rejoice in conquests, either that your power to allure may be seen by other women, or for the pleasure of rousing passionate, feelings that gratify your love of excitement. It must happen, no doubt, that frank and generous women will excite love they do not reciprocate; but, in nine cases out of ten, the woman has, half consciously, done much to excite it. In this case she shall not be held guiltless, either as to the unhappiness or injury of the lover. Pure love, inspired by a worthy object, must ennoble and bless, whether mutual or not; but that which is excited by coquettish attraction, of any grade of refinement, must cause bitterness and doubt as to the reality of human goodness so soon as the flush of passion is over. And that you may avoid all taste for these false pleasures,

"steep the soul In one pure love, and it will last thee long."

The love of truth, the love of excellence, whether or not you clothe them in the person of a special object, will have power to save you much of evil, and lead you into the green glades where the feet of the virtuous have trod. Preserve the modesty of your sex by filling the mind with noble desires, that shall ward off the corruptions of vanity and idleness. "A profligate woman, who left her accustomed haunts and took service in a New York boarding-house, said, 'She had never heard talk so vile at the Five Points as from the ladies at the boarding-house.' And why? Because they were idle; because, having nothing worthy to engage them, they dwelt, with unnatural curiosity, on the ill they dared not go to see." This seems like an exaggeration. Yet Margaret Fuller is responsible for the utterance.[A] Avoid idleness. The mind, like a mill, must have some thought in the hopper of reflection, or the machinery will prove to be self-destructive. Shun flattery. The woman who permits in her life the alloy of vanity; who lives upon flattery, coarse or fine, is lost, and loses the tribute paid the woman by the iron-handed warrior, whom he rejoiced to recognize as his helpmeet, saying, "Whom God loves, to him he gives such a wife."

[Footnote A: Woman of the Nineteenth Century, p. 168.]

The influence of married women over their younger sisters may be beneficent and good. It often is pernicious and bad. Young women judge of men very much by what married women say concerning men. If they speak of men as virtuous and pure, as noble and generous; if they can talk of their husbands as of men who have honored them with their love, and whose kindness blesses their daily life, then will the maiden of a pure heart believe that her dream is real, and that the man of her choice is pure; whose heart is free and open as her own; all of whose thoughts may be avowed; who is incapable of wronging the innocent, or still further degrading the fallen,—a man, in short, whose brute nature is entirely subject to the impulses of his better self. Such men there are in countless numbers, who have kept themselves free from stain, and who can look the purest maiden in the eye and not shun the glance. Through God's grace they have been saved from the path full of peril, and desire nothing more than to share the confidence and friendship of the pure. If, on the other hand, the unmarried are assured by the married that, "if they knew men as they do,"—that is, by being married to them,—"they would not expect continence or self-government from them;" if mothers permit their daughters to mingle freely with the dissipated and vile because of rank or wealth, and when warned that such are not fit companions for a chaste being, reply, "All men are bad sometimes in their life; but give them a pure wife and a home and they will not want to go wrong," then be not surprised if homes are converted into abodes of perpetual sorrow, if not of shame, and the fair young bride is left to weep over the sacrifice of virtue, of honor, and of love, on the altar of an unholy passion. The influence of a pure woman over young women is invaluable.

"Do not forget the unfortunates who dare not cross your guarded way. If it do not suit you to act with those who have organized measures of reform, then hold not yourself excused from acting in private. Seek out these degraded women, give them then tender sympathy, counsel, employment. Take the place of mothers, such as might have saved them originally. If you can do little for those already under the ban of the world,—and the best considered efforts have often failed, from a want of strength in those unhappy ones to bear up against the sting of shame and the frigidness of the world, which makes them seek oblivion again in their old excitements,— you will at least leave a germ of love and justice in their hearts, that will prevent their becoming utterly embittered and corrupt." And you may learn the preventives for those yet uninjured. These will be found in a diffusion of mental culture, simple tastes, best brought by your example, a genuine self-respect, and, above all, the love and fear of a divine in preference to a human tribunal. Let woman live for God and the development of her higher nature,—live so that she can be self helped, as well as helping,—then if she finds what she needs in man embodied, she will know how to love, and be worthy of being loved. Much is said about the underpay of woman as a cause of temptation. It is for the interests of society that there should be an equality of compensation wherever there is an equality of distribution. It is well for woman to ask herself if she is ready to assume the burdens that come from an equality of compensation, such as giving up the prospect of marriage, or of sharing with man the toil of the field, of the factory, as well as of the house. Would woman be willing to take upon herself the responsibility of planning to economize, of building churches, railroads, of entering into a competition with man?—Woman is dependent, not independent.—For this reason man toils to keep his wife, and is ashamed to have his wife keep him. His pride lies in having his home a joy and his wife a helpmeet, rather than to have his wife a rival and his home empty of happiness.

It is not alone by an excess of passion or of beauty that woman becomes a tempter. The absence of love, and of beauty, sins of omission as well as sins of commission, are sources of temptation. Man desires an educated woman. Intellectually and spiritually she must be able to meet his wants, and render help, or she is a failure. He tires of a useless toy or plaything, and cries out for a helpmeet. Another has said, "The bad housekeeping, and the neglect of domestic duties, on the part of many wives, is, no doubt, attributable to the slovenly tenements, and inadequate providings, and careless neglect of the husbands. But more husbands, we fear, are driven to shiftlessness and discouragement—driven to the saloon and gambling-room —by the extravagance or inefficiency, the disorderly arrangements or badly prepared food, the irritating complaints or exacting demands of those who preside in the home. None but a man of low instinct, of base passion, of weak character, will turn away from and neglect a home where order reigns, where a cheerful smile, well-prepared food, neatly arranged table await him; where a word of cheer greets him, and where patient forbearance is exercised, even with his irregularities and faults. It is the part of woman to win; and her winning arts should not be laid aside when she grasps what she has considered a prize. She should seek in every way to win, beyond the possibility of loss, the abiding love, the unwavering confidence, the undoubting respect of her husband. If woman would be man's equal, she must challenge the equality by proving herself mistress of those arts that minister the highest comfort to his physical nature, as well as to his affections, that further his interests as well as his happiness."

Alas! how many fail here because they know not how to make a home pleasant. Such are the slaves of servants and the creatures of circumstances. In some cases the fault is man's, in others it is woman's. Perhaps in all cases both are somewhat at fault; yet the responsibility rests on woman to make home a delight. When she fails she must take the consequences. Failure with her is often a mistake. She knows no better. Ignorance, in some, is wilful, but in more it is educational. Their mothers, through ill-judged kindness, mistaken notions of life, or careless neglect, suffered them to grow up without the necessary practical training; or else they failed before them; and inefficiency and slatternliness, bad cooking, and worse manners, are the patrimony bequeathed in perpetuity to the daughters. Happy is the man who has a wife capable of getting a better meal than the hired help, and whose smile is the light of his dwelling! Sometimes a girl knows how to win, but cares not to keep. She gives place in her heart, and a welcome in her home, to others more readily than to the one she has given her plighted troth. This is criminal. A woman who does it is a suicide. She is bent on ruin, and will find the pit ere long.

Consider her wiles of speech. Mystery here brings ruin to man as it brought ruin to woman. Young ladies of culture and of refinement are not ashamed to employ the language of the Parisian to lead astray the companion of her life. God curse the language and the forms of speech whose words drop with the very gall of death, which revel in elegant dress as near the edge of indecency as is possible without treading over the boundary! Her wiles of speech are bad, but her wiles of love are the most perilous of all. Man needs love. He is fond of it. It is his joy, come from whence it may. Love is the mind's light and heat. A mind of the greatest stature, without love, is like a huge pyramid of Egypt—chill and cheerless in all its dark halls and passages. A mind with love, is as a king's palace lighted for a royal festival. Shame that the sweetest of all the mind's attributes should be suborned to sin. Think of it! each wile, rightly used, is a power given to woman to make her man's helpmeet, and wrongly used will make her man's destroyer.

Some one asked a minister for his conception of the personal appearance of the devil. His reply was, "A false-hearted and well-dressed gentleman, or a vain and fashionable woman." Woman was Satan's first ally, though he worked in ambush, and approached man in concealment. In the wisdom of his choice we discover the peril of woman. It may be well briefly to review the public manner in which Satan employs her talent for the ruin of man and in opposing the rule of Christ.

1. Passing over her social power, and without referring to her wiles of speech, of dress, of flattery, and of love, think of her in the arena of politics, joining her forces to infidelity, and with the disbelievers of the Bible, to obtain for woman a place for which she is not fitted, and which will destroy her peace, injure and undermine her influence in the home, and cause her to neglect wifehood and motherhood, to turn from the interior world of a quiet home, to the outside world of conflict and strife. It is the boast of a writer in favor of "Woman's Rights," that "among the disbelievers of revealed religion, I have not found, during a life of half a century, a single opponent to the doctrine of equal rights for males and females." The correctness of

this statement is to a wonderful extent true. The believers of the Bible claim that the teachings and commands of the Word of God are in opposition to the doctrine. When woman joins the ranks of the infidel, she turns from God, and loses her power in her former sphere.

2. If there is one foe more than another, that threatens us as a nation, nearly all agree in pronouncing that foe to be Romanism. Take this fact in connection with the obvious truth, that it is fashionable to pander to Rome. Because of this tendency ripening into results, the State of New York, politically, is lost to Protestantism, and is as much Roman Catholic as is Italy or Rome. Whence comes this influence, or producing cause? Can we trace it to woman? It will be admitted that the influence of Roman Catholic servants in our homes has never been measured. The nurse teaches the child the use of the beads, and familiarizes the child, committed to her keeping, to the cross, as an emblem of worship. Imagine the alarm of a Christian mother, when, because of the absence of the nurse it became a necessity to see the child to bed, when, to her surprise, the little girl of five years pulled out from beneath the pillow her beads and cross, and began going through the Papal forms of worship! The mother wisely forbore a rebuke, changed her nurse, and led her child back to Christ, and so rescued her. How many children are finding in their nurses, rather than in their mothers, their religious teachers? The influence of Romish servants in our homes is felt in still another way. Because of them there is a barrier to discussion, or even to conversation, concerning this monstrous error, which, like the frogs of Egypt, invades our very bread-troughs. No man dare express his mind concerning Romanism at his table if the servant is a Romanist, lest he lose the services so much in demand, or lest he be reported to the priest, and so be placed under the ban or the displeasure of the Church of Rome, which is used as an engine of political and social power against the truth as it is in Jesus.

3. The influence of education deserves consideration. Fashionable women send their daughters to Roman Catholic institutions of learning, where the Sister or Mother Superior carries her to the chapel, bows reverently before the altar, and kissing the cross, exclaims, "How can Protestants be so blind as to reject the cross on the ground that it savors of Popery, when they know that all their own hopes of salvation must hang upon it?" or where the morning service concludes with a prayer to the "Mother of God," in these words: "Most holy Virgin, I believe and confess thy most holy and immaculate care of man, pure and without stain. O most pure Virgin, through thy virginal purity, thy immaculate conception, thy glorious quality of Mother of God, obtain for me of thy dear Son, humility, charity, great purity of heart, of body and of mind, holy perseverance in my cherished relations, the gift of prayer, a holy life and a happy death."[A] Thus is the dogma of the Immaculate Conception thrust upon the memory, and the gate is opened to a denial and rejection of Christ as the Saviour, and to an acceptance of Mary as the Intercessor. The result manifests itself in two ways. The fashionable boarding-school girl comes to think kindly of Rome, and rebukes all opposition to the church as bigotry or ignorance on the part of those with whom she associates. The influence is noticeable. It is fashionable to attend the Papal Church, fashionable to contribute to its prosperity, fashionable for men to smother their opinions, fashionable for the politician to seek the favor of that power that furnishes, in its subtlety and in its power to work in darkness, a perfect mechanism for Satan.

[Footnote A: Miss Bunkley's Book, pp. 22 and 68.]

4. Our wealthy women, by their patronage of Roman Catholic fairs, and by their gifts to the so-called charitable fund, enable the enemies of the cross of Christ to build these magnificent cathedrals and religious establishments, while the churches of Christ languish for support.

Give to woman the ballot, let these girls in our kitchens become voters, and it will not be difficult to understand how "a man's foes shall be those of his own household."

The Remedy. Induce Protestant girls to work, by treating them as sisters rather than as servants. Talk free in the house and at the table against Romanism, let the consequences be what they may. Educate children so that they shall know the characteristics of this lifelong foe of the church of Christ; and, lastly, resist this movement to change the order of God's government in the home and in the state.

Ignore it as we may, the beguiling serpent is busy with our Eve in America, this Eden of liberty, and God only knows the result. It is a question which cannot be trifled with. That the drift to-day is against the teachings of the Bible, none can doubt. Victory for Satan is a terrible calamity for humanity. Let us then, as an antidote, preach Christ, and strive to make woman the helpmeet of man and the ally of our Divine Master, and then she becomes the deadliest foe of Satan, and the most aggressive champion of the truth.

> "Her rash hand, in evil hour,
> Forth reaching to the fruit, she plucked, she ate!
> Earth felt the wound, and nature from her seat,
> Sighing through all her works, gave signs of woe
> That all was lost."

MILTON.

THE GLORY OF MOTHERHOOD.

To understand the tragedies of the present, it is essential that we re-read the tragedies of the past. Too many, in forming their opinions of what should be, ignore in their calculations what has been, and what must be. Those who are dissatisfied with the position assigned to woman, must recall the fact that God's decrees are unchangeable. We may resist them, but we cannot destroy them. They were in existence, before our birth; they will survive our dissolution. It is for us to recognize God as Ruler as well as Creator, and adjust our views, our lives, and our labors in accordance with an infinitely wise system, formed in the counsels of an eternity past, and running on to the eternity of the future.

If we speak of Woman as God Made Her, of Woman as a Helpmeet, we find a warrant for it in the Word of God. In Eden she was God's ally. When she fell, she became, in sin, the ally of Satan. The truth may be unpalatable, but it is the truth.

In considering woman as a mother, we stand on the hill-top of the past. Before us lies a valley, stretching on from the ruin wrought in Eden by sin, to the restoration wrought in the world by Christ. During these ages of wickedness, of sorrow, and of crime, woman felt the curse heavy upon her. She was made to feel that the *woe* pronounced upon her was a fact; and yet, during all these ages of trial, there was a gleam of hope shining into her soul, because God said, "And I will put enmity between thee and the woman, and between thy seed and her seed; he shall bruise thee on the head, and thou shalt bruise him on the heel." Thus there came to woman, who had the first encounter with the wily enemy of the race, the hope of a triumph over, and a subjugation of this enemy, through her offspring. It is an instinct of a boy to crush the head of a snake; but you cannot readily get a girl to do so: she will run from the beast so identified with her sorrow. The reason for this is explained in the prophecy of Eden. In a mystical sense, Christ, the deliverer foretold in Genesis, the eminent seed of the woman, was to bruise the head of the "old serpent, the devil," that is, destroy him, and all his principalities and powers, break and confound all his schemes and ruin all his works, crush his whole empire, strip him of his sovereignty and authority, of his power over death, and his tyranny over the bodies and souls of men. Here, then, was a purpose worth living for and suffering for. True, Satan, or the serpent, is to bruise his heel, or wound his human nature; but there is no promise of his triumph.

It is not difficult to discover how this hope must have thrilled the heart of Eve with joy. Her life was not to be a failure. Though clouds might rest upon her, it was impossible to shut out the fact that the star of hope was soon to rise, and to usher in the dawn of a glorious day.

Much has been written against the fact that a daughter is not prized in a home as much as is a son. We can understand it, when we go back to Eden and see that the seed of the woman, called "*a he*," a male child, was to be the instrument of working out the disinthralment of the race. The feminine gender is sometimes used in declaring the glories of the future. Zion is called a bride, but her glory is all reflected from the bridegroom. Woman is a helpmeet, but the king-bearer is the man Christ Jesus. The world turned from Christ because he had the appearance of a man. It was a great mistake. It is not a popular saying,—women say it is not complimentary to them to declare it,—yet it remains true, that "God draws by the cords of a man." All along the past men have been recognized as the gift of God. Women rejoice when a man is born into the world; not that women are disliked, but because there is something involved in life more than mere existence. There are faint foreshadowings of the tasks laid on the race. Work is to be done for God and man. Principalities and powers are to be fought and overcome. An invisible world is in league against the race, and an invisible God, once robed in flesh, and living among men, is Our Advocate with God, our Redeemer and Saviour. There is significance in the language, "I have gotten a man from the Lord." The language of Eve, as a mother, furnishes the key-note to that maternal song which yet floats through the world, which makes women in China, in India, in Africa, and in South America, among the inhabitants of Russia, and of Paraguay, anywhere and everywhere, rejoice with the same old joy, when a man is born into the world, because then she feels that somehow she has given birth to a hero and a champion who shall be identified with that song of world-triumph which is yet to cover the earth as the waters cover the sea; and the only exception to this is found among the Hebrews, where a virgin was revered as the possible mother of the Messiah, and so received her dignity as a reflection from the man. To understand this problem of human nature, we must go back to God, and study his word. Those who reject the Word, of God are surrounded by mysteries which they cannot solve. They behold tendencies, and instincts, and dispositions, which are explained in Genesis, and which are parts of God's prophesies yet to be fulfilled in this world. Ignoring the prophecy, they cannot comprehend the facts of existence, which must exist and will exist, whether men will hear or forbear.

Says a writer of some note, "The severe Nation which taught that the happiness of the race was forfeited through the fault of a woman, showed its thought of what sort of regard man viewed her, by making him accuse her in the first question to his God,—who gave her to the patriarch as a handmaid, and by the Mosaical law bound her to allegiance like a serf,—

even they greeted, with a solemn rapture, all great and holy-women as heroines, prophetesses, judges in Israel; and if they made Eve listen to the serpent, gave Mary as a bride to the Holy Spirit. In other nations it has been the same down to our day." In this extract, the Jewish nation and the Bible are referred to in the same tone that we refer to Mahommedans and to the Koran. Is not this tendency perceptible elsewhere? In looking at woman, we ignore the Bible, and God, and history, and talk of her as though the past had no influence with the present and future. The Bible, God, and history have to do with the present and the future, and whoever studies history has been compelled to recognize the truth. This same writer was compelled to declare, "It is the destiny of man, in the course of the ages, to ascertan and fulfil the law of his being, so that his life shall be seen, as a whole, to be that of an angel or messenger." This is his destiny, because it is God-given. Hence man was the bearer of good tidings all along the past. Prophets were generally men. Christ was a man. The apostles, Christ's chosen standard-bearers, were men. The powers in the moral and spiritual world are men. All that is great in history, all that thrones one nation upon a mountain height and buries another in the fathomless grave of infamy, comes from man. The ages were dark, because of the lack of a man. Christ came, and the apostolic age became the noontime of the world, not because of what the race did for themselves, but because of what was done for the race. If a nation sinks, because the man who has the brain, the wisdom, the power from God, is wanting, who shall build up a people in hope, inspire them with grand resolves? It will rise and prosper when the man comes. Christ was a necessity, because infinite work was to be performed. Is he not a necessity now? Is it not a man in Christ, and with Christ, who is ever the worker on the earth? Christ speaks through the gospel, and "the key" of the moral universe is still upon his shoulders. This hope and dream came to Eve way back there in the confines of the wilderness, and so incidentally as well as actually, she became identified with it, and rejoiced when she could declare, "I have gotten a man from the Lord," whom she believed to be the *"promised seed."*

Notice, to Eve, as to woman now, a baby was more than a little child; she saw in him all the possibilities of a man, who was to become a foe worthy to meet the enemy of her soul. Her faith in this child to be born was similar to our faith in the Child that was born in Bethlehem. Hence her joy when she exclaimed, "I have gotten a man from the Lord."

It will seem to many as singular that there should be no mention of the daughters born of Eve. The generations or names of men are given, but not of the daughters. Even there and then the custom now prevalent in the East found its origin. No account is made of the birth of a daughter in that land. Congratulate a man upon the accession to the family of a daughter, and the father will hide his shame with difficulty, and exclaim, "O, that God had given me a son!"

Again, in reading this story some will be surprised to find no mention made of the mother's grief when her youngest child was slain, and that no mention is made of the mother's death. We know that after Seth was born, Adam lived eight hundred years, and begat sons and daughters; but woman's curse bore fruit. Men ruled over her, and her individuality was lost in the headship of Adam. Do not blame me for saying it; I simply declare the fact. This state of things continued until Christ came. When Mary gave birth to Jesus, woman resumed her place. The curse was met by its antidote. From God came the wave of influence which met the wave that flowed out from Eden, the conflict began, higher and higher rose the flood, until the ark of hope by it was placed on the mountain peak of human history, in sight of all races, and tribes, and peoples of the whole world. Calvary is set over against Ararat, as Mary is set over against Eve. After the birth-song of Eden came the tragedy, in which Abel lost his life and Cain his character.

After the birth-song of Bethlehem came the tragedy of Calvary, in which Christ gave up his life, that he might open to man, enveloped in the ruins of the fall, a way back to the Eden in reserve for the redeemed.

In speaking of Eve as a mother, there is little that can be said founded on fact. Eve passes from sight, though the prophecy, "And I will put enmity between thee and the woman, and between thy seed and her seed; he shall bruise thee on the head, and thou shall bruise him on the heel," worked on, and lived on, and found its fulfilment in the triumph won by Christ. It is certainly significant, that Eve, through whom sin came, should pass out of the world's mind, and Mary, through whom Christ came, should vault to a seat in the affections of a world? Is it not also significant that Mary should become an object of worship to many millions of people in this and in other lands, and that Satan, through Mariolatry, should strive to do in the New Dispensation what he wrought by Idolatry in the Old? The opposition of Satan runs on. The purposes of God run on. The prophesies of the Word of God abide, and are sure of fulfilment, in spite of Satan. Against prophecy combinations of men and nations have united; but the truths sweep on resistlessly, and reach the destination for which God ordained them.

The curse that came to woman in the hour of her fall rested on her until Christ came. "Unto thy husband shall be thy desire,"—an expression of subordination and dependence. "He shall rule over thee," expresses the general effect of the apostasy on woman's relations in the married state. The stronger party in this relation, instead of being the guardian and protector of the weaker, did use his superior power to oppress and debase her. Such has always been the case, except so far as the influence of revelation has counteracted the evils of the fall, such is the case to-day. Woman owes her recognition to Christ, and she is indebted for her position in the civilized portions of the world wholly to the gospel. Wherever Christ is not worshipped woman is despised.

Woman as a mother, under the Old Dispensation, differs in many important respects from woman as a mother under the New. The history of woman is divided into three portions: 1. Woman as God made her; 2. Woman as Sin made her; 3. Woman as Christ made her.

1. The position of woman, between her humiliation in Eden and her restoration in Bethlehem, was in many respects sad to contemplate. She was more of a slave than an equal. Eve passes, unrecognized and unnamed, to her grave. Sarah, the wife of Abram, finds mention, and is described in such a manner that you behold her sharing her husband's love, though the picture of her in the home is not a pleasant one. We can hardly understand how Abram could have suffered her to enter the house of Abimelech, nor how she could have taken Hagar to her husband, and thus again have led man astray—the man whom God called to be the Father of the Faithful. Eve, the mother of the race, tempted Adam, and Sarah, the mother of the patriarchs, tempted Abram; and lack of faith in God was the cause of their ruin, and consequent humiliation. There is something sad about the manner of her life. Her home was a simple tent, surrounded by flocks and herds, and crowded with rubbish of every description. Woman in the East is very much to-day what Adam saw her on his first entrance into the wilderness. The effects of sin followed her from generation to generation. The gloom of the night is still over her as she spends her days in out-door labor. She weeds the cotton, and assists in pruning the vine and gathering the grapes. She goes forth in the morning, bearing not only her implements of husbandry, but also her babes in the cradle; and returning in the evening, she prepares her husband's supper and sets it before him, but never thinks of eating of it until after he is done. One of the early objections the Nestorians made to the Female Seminary was, that it would disqualify their daughters for their accustomed toil. In after years woman might be seen carrying her Spelling-book to the field along with her Persian hoe, little dreaming that she was

thus taking the first step towards the substitution of the new implement for the old.

Nestorian parents used to consider the birth of a daughter a great calamity. When asked the number of their children, they would count up their sons, and make no mention of their daughters. The birth of a son was an occasion for great joy and giving of gifts. Neighbors hastened to congratulate the happy father, but days might elapse before the neighborhood knew of the birth of a daughter. It was deemed highly improper to inquire after the health of a wife, and the nearest approach to it was to ask after the house or household. Formerly a man never called his wife by name, but in speaking of her would say the mother of "so and so," giving the name of the child; or the daughter of "so and so," giving the name of her father; or simply that woman did this or that. Nor did the wife presume to call her husband's name, or to address him in the presence of his parents, who, it will be borne in mind, lived in the same apartment. They were married very young, often at the age of fourteen, and without any consultation of their own preference, either as to time or person.

There was hardly a man among the Nestorians who did not beat his wife when the missionaries commenced their labors. The women expected to be beaten, and took it as a matter of course. When the men wished to talk together of anything important, they usually sent the women out of doors or to the stable, as unable to understand or unfit to be trusted. In some cases, says the author of "Woman and Her Saviour," this might be a necessary precaution; for the absence of true affection, and the frequency of domestic broils, rendered the wife an unsafe depositary of any important family affair.[A]

[Footnote A: Woman and her Saviour, pp. 18 and 19.]

In Paraguay a female child is described by Southey as lamenting, in heart-breaking tones, that her mother did not kill her when she was born; and Sir A. Mackenzie declares that there is a class of women in the north who performed this pious duty towards female infants, whenever they had an opportunity. But wherever Christ is known and loved, the daughter is a gift of God as well as a son. Woman owes to her Saviour all she has of joy in time, as well as all she has of hope in eternity. Though she does not obtain the headship, though her sorrow and her pain are not removed, though her desire continues to be to her husband, and though the rule of the husband continues in every well-regulated home, yet woman is elevated to become a shareholder of the pleasures of the home, of the honors and emoluments of life, of the riches obtained by toil, and of the enjoyments derived from culture. Woman in the Christian home is the soul, the pride, the ornament, and the helper. Through Christ she obtains a recognition, so that when we speak of man we mean the race, men and women, for these become the two halves of one thought, so that no especial stress is laid on the welfare of either, but the development of one is secured by the development of the other. To such an extent have the disabilities been removed from the sex, that a leading writer has been compelled to admit, that "in our own country, women are, in many respects, better situated than the men. Good books are allowed, with more time to read them. They are not so early forced into the bustle of life, nor so weighed down by demands for outward success. They have time to think, and no traditions chain them, and few conventionalities, compared with what must be met in other nations. Doors swing open to them, and they are invited to walk the fields of literary and artistic success, and whatever tends to the development of their higher nature is freely placed within their reach."

2. *The trials of motherhood deserve notice.* We have seen the hopes that came to Eve, and beheld their realization in and through Christ. The trials were born of sin. Eve's eldest child, Cain, possessed a narrow, selfish

nature. He was a tiller of the ground. Abel was a keeper of the sheep. The first born met this curse in the soil. The second born looked forward to the restoration. In process of time Cain brought of the fruit of the ground. Tradition has it that he brought what was left of his food, of light and tempting things, flax or hemp seed.

Abel brought of the firstlings of his flock, which was a proper type of Christ. His offering pleased God, Cain's niggardly gift displeased God. The selfish man wreaked his vengeance in the usual way. He slew his brother, who was better than himself. The heavens are black with gathering gloom. Murder is in the air. The shock is felt everywhere. God comes, and sternly asks, "*Where is thy brother?*" Cain impudently replies, "Am I my brother's keeper?" Then comes the curse. It is a self-invited curse, for the gift he gave to God is the harvest in future for himself. Ah, what a lesson. How early it is taught. If you hate God, if you regret what you give, if you make it small, if you see to it that you give the leavings rather than the firstlings, then beware. Cain said his punishment was greater than he could bear. He is getting back what he gave. The command is, Give, and it shall be given back. The converse is true—Keep, and it shall be kept back.

The hopes of Eve were centred in the victory to be achieved over the enemy of her life, by means of the triumph to be won by her children. Her trials really began when she saw that sin was not an accident. It was rebellion which bore fruit. Her treachery to God came back to her in this treachery of her first born to her second child, whom she loved with maternal tenderness. Thus the gates of evil were thrown open, and they filled the land with violence, and the flood became a necessity.

What was true of Eve was more or less true of woman until Christ came. She inherited sorrow, and was born to a life of humiliation and wretchedness. The history of woman in the olden time and at this hour, wherever Christ is not known, is full of sorrow. In Christ she finds an emancipator from sorrow.

There is another strange fact. In the Old Dispensation, the first born son is the child of promise. But wherever the influence of Christ's gospel rules, there the rule of the first born disappears, and all, both sons and daughters, share in the patrimony of the house and in the honors of the household. Despite this, it is natural for a father to love his first born son the best, and for the mother to find her heart clinging involuntarily to the younger and weaker. From the unfortunate the father may turn, but the mother never. She will bind her love tightest about the birdling that, from some misfortune, is unable to leave the maternal nest.

Turn we to the Old Testament, we find that whenever man was brought near to God, as was Abram, Isaac, Jacob, Joseph, and others, woman was held in respect, and was permitted to exercise an elevating influence in the home; and yet it remains true, that in nearly every instance she failed to prove herself a helpmeet.

Sarah introduced Abraham to polygamy, Rebekah was a pattern of lying, and Rachel of deception. The three celebrated women of history are destitute of those characteristics which make of a wife a companion, counsellor, and friend.

Do we study the history of Miriam, of Deborah, and Esther? we behold women rising up in the name of God to help their people to save their kindred. They were the introduction to a noble succession. Woman then, as now, is loved for bringing *help* to those on whom God devolves responsibility.

The picture best loved and most praised in the Old Testament is that of Hannah, the mother of Samuel, as she fits him for his post of duty in the service of the Lord. In Hannah the world finds their beau ideal of a mother, actuated by principle and ruled by love, recognizing her allegiance to God, and her obligations to her child and husband, and there is hardly a child in this Christian land who does not dwell with delight upon this fact, that each year the mother made for her boy a little coat. It was a motherly deed, and links her to the history of the race by the blessed tie which finds its origin in maternal care.

Ruth comes next, because of her fidelity to her mother, and her love of virtue. It is by her life we are introduced afresh to the golden vein of prophecy that runs through the Old Testament, and which ever pointed towards the coming of Christ as the hope of woman and the hope of the world. Esther's love of her race, and her noble daring of Eastern despotism for the good of her people, lifts her to a high place, though as a wife and mother we know nothing more than that she was hedged round by the iron regulations of a paganized court. The revelations made concerning the daughter of Jacob, or of Bathsheba, the loved wife of David, and in fact of nearly all of the women of the Bible, prove that the women of the olden time left as well as received an inheritance of shame. The names we have mentioned are among the brightest and the best. We will draw a veil over the characters of women such as the wife of Lot, or of Potiphar, the would-be seducer of Joseph, or of Job, the betrayer of her husband in misfortune, of Jezebel, the fury, or of Delilah, the traitress to her husband, and of a score of others, that make the age in which they lived seem like the night of humanity.

3. *Woman obtains her recognition in Christ.* From the moment God pronounced sentence upon Eve to the moment when the angel appeared to Mary, man was recognized as the head. Even Miriam wrought through Moses, and Deborah, the judge and prophetess, lays no claim to personal communication with God, but quotes his promises, and stimulates Barak to action, So also when the angel came from the court of heaven to foretell the joy that was to come to the world in the birth of John, the forerunner of Christ, he came to Zacharias instead of to Elisabeth. But when the message related to Christ, *then the angel passed by man, and approached woman direct.* God never forgets. A thousand years are but as a day to Him. Yesterday, in Eden, he foretold the coming of Christ to Eve. To-day, in Nazareth, the angel comes to Mary, and makes her heart glad with the fact, that she was chosen to become the mother of our Lord. Eve lost by sin God's companionship. Mary obtained, through Christ, favor with God and man. The valley is spanned with this arch of hope. The night of woman's humiliation is passing away. And the angel came in unto her, and said, "Hail, thou that art highly favored, the Lord is with thee; blessed art thou among women."

Strange words these, as we can readily perceive, from the position held by woman previously. No wonder that when she saw him, she was troubled at his saying, and cast in her mind what manner of salutation this should be. And the angel said unto her, "Fear not, Mary, for thou hast found favor with God. And behold, thou shall conceive in thy womb, and bring forth a son, and shall call his name Jesus. He shall be great, and shall be called the Son of the Highest; and the Lord God shall give unto him the throne of his father David, and he shall reign over the house of Jacob forever, and of his kingdom there shall be no end." No wonder that the air seemed full of music. Woman, made so beautiful, woman, so beloved of God, and so prized by Adam, before sin blighted the bud of hope and spoiled the flower of beauty, was now to come forth from the darkness and gloom of her life of shame to the light of an unclouded day, henceforth to be made glorious by her ministrations of love. The glory of motherhood "is the man gotten from the Lord," and raised to work for God in this sinful world. The glory of woman is to share this man's home as a helpmeet, and contribute by her love, and sympathy, and efforts to his happiness and usefulness here, that she may wear the crown of joy in heaven.

MARIOLATRY NOT OF CHRIST.

If ever woman had reason to sing, "My spirit hath rejoiced in God my Saviour," it was Mary, the Virgin Mother of Christ. God recognized her as a helper in restoring man from the ruins of sin. To her the angel spake, saying, "Hail, thou that art highly favored. The Lord is with thee. Blessed art thou among women." And in pondering in her heart the strange coincidences, she exclaimed, "God hath regarded the low estate of his handmaiden; for behold from henceforth all generations shall call me blessed."

From these words it is evident that Mary appreciated the honor conferred upon her by her Creator and rightful Ruler. It is a singular fact, that Eve, betrayed by Satan, betrayed the race. Mary held steadfast to God and to truth; and yet Satan has the second time taken woman and used her as an ally, and so has brought an influence to bear upon the minds of men which has led millions astray, and covers vast portions of the world with the gloom of a moral night. Mary, the "Mother of Jesus," is made to take the place of "Christ, the Son of God," and is declared to be the Mother of God. In this land we can form no conception of the extent to which this worship of Mary is carried in Roman Catholic countries. To the Italians Mary is God, and worship is simply the adoration of the Virgin. Viewing Romanism in the light of the Bible, this is its crowning sin; viewing it as a system combined to seduce and enslave, this is its masterpiece. To understand how it is so, let us think how deep in man's nature is placed the feeling of the need of a being like unto himself, to mediate between him and God. The Bible completely meets this want in the God-man. But Popery blots out the God-man as mediator, and in his stead presents us with Mary, who is to the devotee the "one living and true God;" for, though the Father and Son are known, they are accessible only through Mary, and they stand so far behind and beyond her, that to the Romanist they are vague, shadowy, and unknown. Mary is the first name to be lisped in childhood, the last to be uttered by the quivering lips before they are closed in death. Around the neck of the infant is suspended a small image of the Virgin; when the babe seeks the breast it must kiss the image, and thus literally does it draw in the adoration of Mary with its mother's milk. "Were the New Testament to be written at this hour, Rome would blot out the name of Christ and substitute that of Mary. Take a proof: The church close by the Vatican has upon its marble pediment, graven in large letters, 'Let us come to the throne of the Virgin Mary, that we may find grace to help us in our time of need.' The Roman sees Heb. iv. 16 quoted, but cannot verify it if he would, seeing the Bible is forbidden to him." Pius IX., at the foot of the column of the Immaculate Conception, erected to perpetuate the fact that he was permitted to decree the dogma, has Moses, David, Isaiah, and Jeremiah casting crowns before the Virgin, saying, "Thou art worthy; for thou wast slain, and hast redeemed us to God by thy blood." When it was announced that the French occupation of Rome should cease, the Pope published a decree calling on all Rome to go with him to the feet of Mary, if haply by cries and tears they might prevail with her to avert from the throne of God's vicar the dangers that threaten it; and in that act the Pope led the way.[A]

[Footnote A: Minister *versus* Priest, page 7.]

For this worship of the Virgin Mary there is a reason. Satan could not successfully lead astray so many millions of people, despite a preached gospel and a printed Bible, unless there was some truth lying at the root of this ineradicable Virgin worship. This root we shall discover when we recall woman's position prior to the advent of Christ, the place she was called upon to fill in the scheme of redemption, and the influences set in motion by the life of Christ upon the earth.

1. *Let us notice woman's position previous to the advent.* Before Christ came, woman was regarded as inferior to man. She had lost her equality. She was excluded from general intercourse, and her confinement to her own home and apartments, without education, without social recognition, left her without strength of character, self-reliance, or resources with herself. "Woman's safety in society lies in two elements: her own virtue and intelligence, and the consequent respect for her which such a character inspires. Where these two things are found, she may participate in general society, mingling freely with men as their equals, and regarded, it may be, even as their superiors. Here, it may be worthy of note, that no such estimate or honor is ever put upon woman except when Christianity has given her this elevation."

Before Christ appeared, the qualities honored as divine were peculiarly the virtues of the man—courage, wisdom, truth, strength. Womanly virtues were regarded as puerile and contemptible, and woman herself was little better than a slave.

2. *Notice the place woman filled in the scheme of redemption.* It is admitted by those who recognize the Word of God as authority, that the Atonement required the sacrifice of one whose nature represents equally the dignity of the Law-maker and the humanity of the transgressor. In him Deity and humanity must be united: Deity, that he may give value to the offering; humanity, that he may obey the positive precepts and endure the penal sanction of the law human nature has violated. It was therefore

essential that the prophecy of Isaiah, uttered six hundred years before the advent, should be fulfilled, viz., "Behold, a virgin shall conceive and bring forth a son, and they shall call his name Immanuel—God with us." This work had been accomplished, and Mary was honored with the privilege of taking the words of Eve, "I have gotten a man with Jehovah," and making it no longer a prophecy, but a fact. So we sing,—

> "Thou wast born of woman; them didst come,
> O, Holiest! to this world of sin and gloom,
> Not in thy dread omnipotent array;
> And not by thunder strewed
> Was thy tempestuous road,—
> Nor indignation burned before thee on thy way;
> But thou, a soft and naked child,
> Thy mother undefiled,
> In the rude manger laid to rest,
> From off her virgin breast."

Then, for the first time, the mother resumed her place. When the wise men came into the house they saw the young child, with Mary his mother, and fell down and worshipped him; and when they had opened their treasures they presented unto him gifts, gold, and frankincense, and myrrh. The old Eastern custom, which placed the child before the mother, was now understood. God guarded against making Mary first, and at the same time provided for her a place. When God appeared to Joseph in a dream, he did not say, Take the mother and child, but the "young child and his mother, and flee into Egypt." This brings us naturally to consider—

3. *The influences set in motion by the life of Christ upon the earth.* First, let us review the history of Christ's personal relations to Mary. Up to twelve years of age, his home was in Nazareth; and Luke declares (second chapter,

fortieth verse), "The child grew and waxed strong in spirit, filled with wisdom; and the grace of God was upon him. And when he was twelve years old, his parents went up to Jerusalem, after the custom of the feast. And when they had fulfilled the days, as they returned the child Jesus tarried behind in Jerusalem; and Joseph and his mother knew not of it. For three days he was away from them. When they found him he was in the temple, sitting in the midst of the doctors, both hearing them and asking them questions. And all that heard him were astonished at his understanding and answers. And when they saw him, they were amazed: and his mother said unto him, Son, why hast thou thus dealt with us? Behold, thy father and I have sought thee sorrowing."

It is noticeable that Luke mentions Joseph before he mentions the mother; and when Mary speaks, she ignores the miraculous conception, and calls him the son of Joseph. But Jesus *does not forget* his origin, nor does he recognize Joseph as father, but says, How is it that ye sought me? Wist ye not that I must be about my Father's business? And they understood not the saying he spake unto them. And he went down with them, and came to Nazareth, and was subject unto them; but his mother kept all these sayings in her heart. "And Jesus increased in wisdom and stature, and in favor with God and man."—Luke ii. 42.

Again, at Cana of Galilee, there was a marriage, and the mother of Jesus was there. Eighteen years have passed since we last saw him in the temple, when Mary ignored his miraculous conception, and when Jesus rebuked her, by asserting his Sonship and by claiming God as Father. At Cana both Jesus and his disciples are invited to the wedding. And when they wanted wine, the mother of Jesus saith unto him, They have no wine. Jesus saith unto her, "Woman, what have I to do with thee? Mine hour is not yet come." Plainly, and in the most emphatic manner, Christ refuses to recognize Mary as intercessor or director. A third instance is still more marked. Jesus is talking to an immense multitude, and is making a hand-to-hand fight with Pharisees and Scribes. "While he yet talked to the people, behold, his mother and his brethren stood without, desiring to speak with him." Evidently Mary had no idea of the character or the mission of the Man Christ Jesus, but feeling that he was popular, she was glad to exhibit her relationship in a public manner, and so through the throng sent in word, saying, "Tell Jesus his mother and his brethren stand without, desiring to speak with him." But he answered, and said unto him that told him, "Who is my mother? and who are my brethren?" It is not difficult to picture the God-man shaking off the trammels of the flesh and rising to the height of his great work. What a contrast is presented between the second and the first Adam! The first Adam yielded without remonstrance to Eve, who had worshipped the creature rather than the Creator, and thus paved the way for the introduction of idolatry; while the second Adam—the Lord of Glory—withstood the influences of Mary, rebuked her intermeddling and dictation, and stood forth to his work in the declaration as he Stretched out his hand towards his disciples, and said, "Behold my mother and my brethren. For whosoever shall do the will of my Father who is in heaven, the same is MY BROTHER, AND SISTER, AND MOTHER."

Again, while Christ was conversing with his disciples, a certain woman of the company lifted up her voice, and said unto him, "Blessed is the womb that bore thee, and the paps which thou hast sucked." Thus suddenly flamed up this passion for Mariolatry. It was instantly rebuked by the words, "Yea, rather, blessed are they that hear the Word of God and keep it." Thus he tore the crown from the brow of Mary woven by the irreligious, and intimated that, as Mary was greater than Eve, because of her identification with Himself, so whosoever should believe in Christ, and serve him, should be the equal of Mary. The purpose of God in forming Eve, should be realized in the womanly character resulting from a reception of the truth as it is in Jesus, and by doing the will of God on the earth.

Thus he severed the tie binding him to family, and proclaimed himself the Son of Man, and the Son of God, the Brother of the Faithful. From this declaration came the brotherhood and sisterhood of the church of Christ, so that no matter what be the rank or position of the worldling redeemed by the blood of Christ, he becomes an equal shareholder in love, and is recognized as a partaker in the fellowship of the church.

At the cross we find Mary standing with others. When Jesus therefore saw his mother and the disciple standing by whom he loved, he saith unto his mother, "Woman, behold thy son." Then saith he to the disciple, "Behold thy mother." And from that hour the disciple took her unto his own house. Once more she appeal's as worshipper, and not as the worshipped. Her name is mentioned, with others, in Acts i. 14, as being with the disciples in the Pentecostal chamber waiting for the descent of the Holy Spirit.

From this scriptural testimony, it is apparent that the Saviour, by his conduct towards his mother, shielded the church from the curse of Mariolatry. Had he yielded in one instance, reasons for supporting the claims of Romanism had been furnished. Mary was only a woman. She was honored of God just as far as she served God, and when she turned aside she was no more than any other person. Her perceptions of Christ's work were not as distinct or comprehensive as were those of Mary the sister of Lazarus, or of Mary Magdalene. In this Mary was not peculiar. Very frequently women associated with great workers fail to appreciate the character of the work committed to them to do. To the world a worker may seem to be a wonder. To the one most intimately associated with him he is a very ordinary individual. It is said a man is never a hero to his servant. Is it not almost as true of his wife? A living great man is ordinary in so many things in his daily life, that the wife forgets his greatness. The wife of John Milton saw but a blind man in the bard, dwelling upon his immortal thought and evolving his world-renowned poem. As the eagle stirs up her nest, compelling her broodlings to exert themselves, so God sometimes suffers a good man to link his fortunes with a woman who is ill-mated with him in every way. In the light of the fact that Jesus found little or no appreciation in the society of Mary, and sought the home-joys elsewhere, woman ought to learn a lesson. Is it not possible that you mistake your mission, and strike the rock of stumbling in your home, rather than avoid it by ignoring that which is grand and admirable in the life of him with whom you are associated? Doubtless in a busy man, now full of joy, and now morose; now engrossed by a thought or scheme to such an extent that he forgets himself and his family, and now idle and listless as a boy,—it may be hard, yet it is none the less a duty for woman to love him for what he is, and to see to it that he be ministered unto in his efforts. O, how dear to the heart of a working man—no matter whether he toil with brain or hand—who feels that his wife understands him, defends and protects him, and keeps the home bright with love, though tempests may sweep across the path that leads him into the world! There is a lesson here which belongs to men. Mary's lack of appreciation did not turn Jesus from his work. It permitted his true character to appear to better advantage. It tore down the scaffolding of Mariolatry, and permitted the God-man to stand forth in his grand proportions. "Wist ye not I must be about my Father's business?" said Jesus. Many men make trouble at home an excuse for going to the bad. It is not an excuse. The design of home trouble may be to send a man to Jesus; to make the tendrils of love twine about the heavenly rather than the earthly. It surely is not to induce a man to twine his affections about the devilish and earthly. It is not manly thus to do.

Man moves in three circles. The first is that of Self; the second that of Family; the third that of Country. A man who properly performs duties that pertain to himself, we shall not call noble. By neglecting family he becomes less than a man. By performing them never so well he comes not to merit applause. Distinctive nobleness begins with the third class. It is when he rises above self and family, when he looks abroad on the family of mankind, that he takes the altitude which in a man is distinctively great; when he feels no longer the little necessities which compel, or the little pleasures which allure, and yet is able to contemplate men as a great brotherhood of immortals, with a gaze analogous to Him in whose image he is made; when he can look on the world through the light of eternity, and is willing to suffer all things, and to endure all things, that by him and through him blessings may reach others,—then it is he does that which it is the high privilege of man on this earth to do, and becomes a power to which under God humanity owes all it has achieved in time. "I serve" is the law of the living forces of mankind. Each man and woman has a place. If they fill it, they furnish a channel along which God's beneficent purposes find their way to a lost world. If they do not fill it, they are set aside, and the verdict of the world is, Served them right.

It if surprising that, after Mary had been rebuked at Cana of Galilee, that she should have presumed to have interrupted Jesus in the presence of the multitude. It is instructive that Christ taught us that the tie binding us to God and to humanity, is the most sacred of all; for while it made the God-man a brother to us, it makes us co-workers with God in carrying forward the enterprises with which men are identified on the earth. When a man is true to self, to humanity, and to God, and so girds himself with the strength arising from confidence, he deserves the support, if not the admiration, of those with whom he is associated. It was unworthy of Mary to ignore the Divine origin of Jesus, and call Joseph his father before the elders. She thought to raise herself by lowering him. He would not be lowered. By his mother and by the world he knew that he had a right to be recognized as the Son of God. This tendency to belittle greatness lives yet. Men are seldom known until they die. We praise the dead and ignore the living, as a rule. There is too little respect shown to men occupying positions of public trust.

There is too little respect shown in the household. The father and mother are not honored in the home as they deserve to be, and in the state the same principle rules. "Thou shall not speak evil of the ruler of thy people," is an apostolic precept, and the command, "Honor thy father and thy mother," was repeatedly reiterated by Christ.

It is a significant fact, that Eve was led astray by Satan in the same direction that was Mary. Mariolatry is only the outgrowth of the seedling that lay dormant in Mary's heart, and is indigenous. It is not natural for us to be contented with being used as an instrument for glorifying God. We desire to be honored, as something more than an instrument. In fact, it is true, that all are, no matter what their powers or capacities, instrumentalities employed of God for distinct purposes. Against this power we revolt and are thrust aside. The *really* great delight to recognize this truth, and their prayer is, "Use me for thy glory" and for the world's advantage.

Another truth incidentally appears, and furnishes the root of Mariolatry. We come to appear to the world what we really are. Mary was tempted to place herself above Christ, and so we are not surprised that those who have turned against Christ should join the tempter in placing Mary above her Son. The refutation is the life of Christ, who died for man, and the life of Mary, who never forgot herself in thinking of others. The triumph of Mary was won by submission. Had she revolted against Christ, she had lost all. In the First Epistle of Paul to the Corinthians, the apostle speaks of the glory of the women as of a thing distinct from the glory of the men. They are the two opposite poles of the sphere of humanity. "Their provinces are not the same, but different. The qualities which are beautiful when predominant in one are not beautiful when predominant in the other. That which is the glory of the one is not the glory of the other." The glory of true womanhood is a combination of various qualities, many of which were illustrated by the life of Mary. She was considerate of others. She was submissive. As has been said, "In the very outset of the Bible, submission is revealed as her peculiar lot and destiny. If you were merely to look at the words as they stand declaring the results of the fall, you would be inclined to call that vocation of obedience a curse but in the spirit of Christ it is transformed, like labor, into a blessing." The origin or root of Mariolatry has been accounted for in the following manner: "In all Christian ages the especial glory ascribed to the Virgin Mother is purity of heart and life. Gradually in the history of the Christian church, the recognition of this became idolatry. The works of early Christian art commonly exhibit the progress of this perversion. They show how Mariolatry grew up. The first pictures of the early Christians simply represent the woman. By and by we find outlines of the mother and the child. In an after age, the Son is seen sitting on a throne, with the mother crowned, but sitting, as yet, below him. In an age still later, the crowned mother is on a level with the Son. Later still, the mother is on a throne above the Son. And, lastly, a Romish artist represents the Eternal Son, in wrath, about to destroy the earth, and the Virgin Intercessor interposing, pleading by significant attitudes her maternal rights, and redeeming the world from his vengeance. Such was, in fact, the progress of virgin worship."

First, the woman reverenced for the Son's sake, then the woman reverenced above the Son and adored. This is the history. To account for it, various theories have been advocated. One, assuming it as a principle that no error has ever spread widely that was not the exaggeration or perversion of a truth, finds in the influence exerted by Christ the germ out of which Mariolatry springs. But surely nothing could be farther from what Christ taught. By word, by look, and by action, Christ opposed the debasing and degrading thought. Mariolatry, like idolatry, is the outgrowth of the religion of nature. The carnal heart is at enmity with God. It prefers to worship something besides God, and so in the old dispensation it found its idol in the hero. As the heathen counted for divine the legislative wisdom of the man,—manly strength, manly truth, manly justice, manly courage, Hercules with his club, Jupiter with his thunderbolt, so Baal, representing the primeval power of nature, became the object of idolatrous worship. After Christ, partly because of the new spirit which pervaded the world, and largely because the carnal heart, ruled by Satan, is glad of any pretext to neglect Christ, Mary, the mother, became preferable to Christ the Son. Salvation depends upon faith in Christ. Whosoever believeth in the Son hath everlasting life. For God so loved the world, that he gave his only begotten Son, that whosoever believeth in him should not perish, but have everlasting life. This being true, a belief in Mary as an intercessor is as sinful in God's sight, and is as directly opposed to a faith in Christ, as was a belief in Baal or Jupiter. By whatever means Satan induces men to reject Christ, he ruins them, and destroys their hope of salvation. Satan induced Eve to reject God, to believe in him, and to serve him. There is no evidence that Mary would have consented to occupy the place to which an idolatrous world has raised her, but Satan cares not for that, so that "he may work with all power, and signs, and lying wonders, and with all deceivableness of unrighteousness in them that perish."

The peril arising from the perversion's of biblical truth is illustrated by the history of the diaconate as well as by the history of the motherhood of Jesus. The influences set in motion by the life of Christ deserve to be carefully pondered. Perverted, they have helped on error. Used and employed as Christ designed them, they are subservient of the highest interests of society. Truly has it been said, The life and the cross of Christ shed a splendor from heaven upon a new and till then unheard of order of heroism—that which may be called the feminine order—meekness, endurance, long-suffering, the passive strength of martyrdom. For Christianity does not say, "Honor to the wise," but, "Blessed are the meek." Not "Glory to the strong," but "Blessed are the pure in heart, for they shall see God." Not the Lord is a man of war; Jehovah is his name, but God is love. In Christ, not intellect, but love, is glorified. In Christ is magnified, not force of will, but the glory of a Divine humility. He was obedient unto death, even the death of the cross; wherefore God hath also exalted Him. Therefore it was, that from that time forward, woman assumed a new place in the world. It is not to mere civilization, but to the spirit of life in Christ, that woman owes all she has and all she has yet to gain. In Christ, manly and womanly characteristics were united, and were in equipoise. He was not the Son of the Man, but the Son of Man. It was not manhood, but humanity, that was made divine in him. Humanity has its two sides: one side in the strength and intellect of manhood; the other in the tenderness and faith and submission of womanhood; man and woman, the two halves of one thought, make up human nature. In Christ, not one alone, but both were glorified. Strength and Grace, Wisdom and Love, Courage and Purity,—Divine Manliness, Divine Womanliness. In all noble characters, the two are blended; in Him—the noblest—blended into one entire and perfect humanity. The spirit which pervades the world because of Christ's coming, and of the influence exerted by his Gospel, opens to woman a faith which has been growing clearer and brighter for eighteen centuries. By this we do not affirm or imply that the coming of Christ restored woman to the equality she enjoyed in the morning of creation, or that his coming removed the curse then pronounced upon her. If Christ's coming removed a part of the curse, then it must have removed all, which we know is false; woman still has sorrow in child-bearing, and man earns his daily bread by the sweat of his brow. Christ's coming removed the disabilities from woman. He turned the attention of the world to feminine characteristics, and shed over them the halo of a divine light. He brought the woman up as he lowered the glory hitherto attached to characteristics distinctively manly. Where Christ is loved, the gladiator and prize-fighter are despised, and a meek and quiet spirit is honored. The heart is the seat of power more than the intellect. Blessed are the pure in heart, rather than the great in intellect. Pureness rather than strength is the ideal of the human heart, since Christ was slain. While, then, it is true that the worship of Mary is idolatry, and that the worship given to her is so much taken from Christ, we must not forget that the only glory of the Virgin was the glory of true womanhood. "The glory of true womanhood consists in being herself; not in striving to be something else. It is the false paradox and heresy of this present age to claim for her as a glory, the right to leave her sphere. Her glory lies in her sphere, and God has given her a sphere distinct; as in the Epistle to the Church of Corinth, when, in that wise chapter, St. Paul rendered unto womanhood the things which were woman's, and unto manhood the things which were man's."

Mary's glory was not immaculate origin, nor immaculate life, nor exaltation to Divine honors. She has none of these things. Hers was the glory of simple womanhood. The glory of being true to the nature assigned her by her Maker, the glory of Motherhood; the glory of a meek and quiet spirit, which is, in the sight of God, of great price. For all women there is something nobler than to be recognized as the queen of heaven. Let woman be content to be what God made her, to fill the sphere God appointed for her, in unselfishness, and humbleness, and purity, rejoicing in God her Saviour, content that He had regarded the lowliness of His handmaiden, and rejoicing that God has honored the characteristics regarded as feminine, which she possesses, and which she may use for the glory of God and the good of the race. Now, as in the olden time, it is her privilege to minister unto the necessities of Jesus, by cheerfully contributing of her substance to the support of His cause, and by lavishing her love, upon those qualities of the head and heart, which in Christ appeared in perfected beauty, and are to-day the charm of life, the power of religion, and the glory of Christianity.

WOMAN'S WORK AND WOMAN'S MISSION.

Woman's work is a work of charity. The fact points back to woman's origin. God brought her as a gift to man, with characteristics and endowments which fitted her to be his helpmeet, his counsellor, and companion. Recall Adam's position. He was alone in the garden. He found no helper in the beasts. He longed for a kindred spirit. Endowed with a nature too communicative to be content with itself, he requires society, a resting point, a complement, for he only half lives while he lives alone. Made to speak, to think, to love, his thought seeks another thought to reveal and quicken itself; his speech is lost sorrowfully in the air, or only awakens an echo which reverberates it, but cannot reply; his love knows not where to fix itself, and falling back on itself, threatens to become a barren egotism; in short, fill his being aspires to another self, but his other self does not exist. At this time, when the desire for communion was stifling him, he slept, and from his side God took a rib and made woman, and brought her to him. Behold Adam. He sees her, and is in rapture.

"Grace was in all her steps, heaven in her eye,
In every gesture dignity and love."

Milton describes Adam as saying—

"I now see
Bone of my bone, flesh of my flesh, myself

> Before me; Woman is her name, of man
> Extracted: for this cause he shall forego
> Father and mother, and to his wife adhere;
> And they shall be one flesh, one heart, one soul."

The imagination paints this scene. In fancy we behold Adam winning Eve, "for she would be wooed, and not unsought be won." Won she was, and Adam was brought to the sum of earthly bliss. They dwell together in sweet accord, Adam fears for her safety when apart from him. Evil threatens them. Together they would be strong, he thinks, apart they would be weak, and so in fear he speaks of the enemy lurking in the garden, and seeking to find them asunder.

> "Hopeless to circumvent us joined, where each
> To other speedy aid might lend at need;
> Whether his first design be to withdraw
> Our fealty from God, or to disturb
> Conjugal love, than which, perhaps, no bliss
> Enjoyed by us excites his envy more;
> Or this or worse, leave not the faithful side
> That gave thee being, still shades thee and protects.
> The wife, where danger or dishonor lurks,
> Safest and seemliest by her husband stays,
> Who guards her, or with her the worst endures."

Eve resents the imputation of weakness, and insists on being left forever fancy free to roam at will. In self-confidence she goes forth and falls, and in falling introduces sin into the world.

Let us review the past, and recall a few facts which, deserve consideration, before we enter upon the contemplation of Woman's Work and Woman's Mission. It will not be denied that Eve was created to be a helpmeet. That Satan tempted her, and converted the helpmeet into a tempter. In that light we have considered her power. We have seen that Eve, in bringing ruin to man, turned her back upon the Creator and Preserver of mankind, and paved the way for the introduction of idolatry, the shadows of whose multiplying altars shrouded the old world in the gloom of night. From the ruin of Eve to the restoration in Mary, the history of this world resembles a deep valley filled with death and sorrow and gloom. In Adam all died, in Christ all shall be made alive. Bethlehem with its manger is set over against Eden with its bower. During that old dispensation, manly qualities were honored and womanly qualities were ignored. The effects of sin are seen. God doth not hold guiltless the sinner. The consequences of sin run on. They made woman's life wretched. They changed the helpmeet into a slave. Do not rebel, woman, at the utterance, nor suffer yourself to feel that God does not care for woman, or that he willingly afflicts her.

It is at this point you do well to survey the field. We know that God's purposes run on. That God was not and will not be defeated. That the plan formed in the councils of eternity is sure to be successfully executed.

Hence God's idea of woman is yet to bless the world. What sin destroyed Christ came to restore, and more than to restore. In heaven if not on earth we shall see woman as God made her, and as God glorified her. This brings us to the consideration of what Christ did for her. He did not permit Mary to become Intercessor, and so give a sanction to Mariolatry, which in evil is second only to idolatry. He did not lift woman to the position of ruler, nor did he give any sanction to the wild vagaries of the Christless ones, who are striving to overturn the foundations of society, and who rebel against motherhood, wifehood, and sisterhood; but he did turn the attention of the world towards the graces of womanhood, and while he turned his back upon those manly qualities of labor, of pluck, of brute courage, he turned his face towards meekness, gentleness, and love, and made the vales of life to blossom with a new beauty. He welcomed woman as a companion. He sought her for sympathy's sake, and opened his heart to her in the fullest confidence.

Let us notice this truth. In making woman's work a work of charity, he continued in the New Dispensation the work which was commenced in the Old. He lifted the thread where woman broke it, and reuniting it again sent her forth into the world to bless it with love, with sympathy, with ministrations of tenderness, with an elevating companionship, which makes man worthy of his origin, and helps him to fulfil the mission of God's anointed.

And though Satan has taken this new thought and perverted it, as he has perverted all the rest, and though he has employed the Church of Rome, by organizing women into orders and sisterhoods of charity, so that woman may again be enslaved and destroyed; though the story of her confinement in nunneries and establishments little better in form than prisons, and far more cruel in character, has been written, let us not be discouraged, but believing that Christ's plan is best, let us learn what his will is, and then let us do it in the fear of God and in the love of truth, assured that his ways are higher and better and grander than ours, and that it is safe to trust God even where we cannot trace him, remembering that "he doeth great things, past finding out; yea, and wonders without number."

In considering Woman's Work and Woman's Mission, we discover that they go hand in hand, and faith is the bond which unites them. Separate woman's work from her mission, and you divorce it from that which makes it honorable and praiseworthy. It is the spirit of faith, and love, and hope, and charity, which pervades the life of the true woman, that is her glory and her praise. The difference between woman as a drudge and woman as a helpmeet, describes the relation existing between her work and her mission.

Work separated from this path of faith, love, and charity, becomes unholy to the world and unbearable to her. The holiest of all work for a mother is to care for her child. That child, so helpless now, is to reward her by acts of love and deeds of valor. Take away from woman her faith, let her feel that her work is a degradation, and there is nothing more beautiful in her attentions to a child than there would be in her attentions to a pig.

When in the country the children and their parents were floating in a little boat on a river's surface, they admired the lilies with their white leaves spread out on the wave. After they had looked upon the flower, I asked them to observe the roots, and see in what they were embedded. They replied, "The roots are in the mud." That lily illustrates truthfully the spiritual character of woman's work. Though her life may be passed in drudgery, yet the flower of her life is seen in the neatness, beauty, and comfort of the home, and her joy is derived from the commendation received by her diligence and toil. Truly has the poet told, in this homely way, how

LOVE LIGHTENS LABOR.

    A good wife rose from her bed one morn,
   And thought, with a nervous dread,
  Of the piles of clothes to be washed, and more
   Than a dozen mouths to be fed.
 There were meals to be got for the men in the field,
   And the children to fix away
To school, and the milk to be skimmed and churned;
   And all to be done that day.

    It had rained in the night, and all the wood
   Was wet as it could be,
And there were pudding and pies to bake,

  And a loaf of cake for tea.
The day was hot, and her aching head
  Throbbed wearily as she said—
"If maidens but knew what good wives know,
  They would, be in no hurry to wed."

  "Jennie, what do you think I told Ben Brown?"
  Called the farmer from the well;
And a flush crept up to his bronzed brow,
  And his eye half bashfully fell;
"It was this," he said, and coming near,
  He smiled, and stooping down,
Kissed her cheek—"'twas this, that *you were the best*
  And dearest wife in town!"

  The farmer went back to the field, and the wife,
  In a smiling and absent way,
Sang snatches of tender little songs
  She'd not sung for many a day.
And the pain in her head was gone, and the clothes
  Were white as foam of the sea;
Her bread was light, and her butter was sweet,
  And golden as it could be.

  "Just think," the children all called in a breath,
  "Tom Wood has run off to sea!
He wouldn't, I know, if he only had
  As happy a home as we."
The night came down, and the good wife smiled
To herself, as she softly said,

"'Tis sweet to labor for those we love—
  'Tis not strange that maids will wed!"

There is a glory in motherhood which robes woman in beauty, and fills the home with the light of heaven. The mother, busy with her cares, and attending to the wants of her children, is honored wherever Christ is loved.

Now, because the world links woman's work and mission together, the world is full of pictures of the mother and the child. To a true-hearted man, it is almost impossible to find any picture to which his nature turns with fonder delight than to that of a mother with a child sleeping on the breast, full of sweet trust and enjoying a dreamless repose, or being ministered to in his nude state in the morning bath. The spiritual covers the common with a halo of glory, and robes woman in the light of love.

The same is true of the housewife. In the daily routine of duty, which is essential to the comfort and bliss of home life, there is nothing very attractive in the ordinary occupations of the home. Let a woman attempt the task with no outlook, with no hope. Let her do it for so much money, and nothing more, and she becomes morose, discontented, sad and cheerless. Let her do this for love. Let her feel that she is contributing to some one's joy, or that she is to use the money earned for some worthy purpose, and at once the loftiness of her purpose sanctifies her deed, and renders that which would have been unbecoming, if done without a motive, right and noble when performed under the pressure of a great and noble aspiration, for "'tis sweet to labor for those we love."

Woman's work is defined by her Creator to be a work of charity. She is a helpmeet. A gift she came to man. Her life is a constant giving up of rights and privileges for the happiness of others. She waits on man not for pay, but for love. She ministers to him in sickness and in health. It is not the deed, but the spirit which sanctifies the deed, that makes it lovely. Compel her by force, by fear, or by rewards, to do what she performs because of love, and you destroy all the beauty of the action, and convert the ministering angel into a menial, the God-appointed woman into a brutalized slave. God made her a gift, and the law of her life is in giving. She fulfils the functions of her life by living in harmony with the law of love. The woman, described with such inexpressible tenderness by Luke (vii. 37-50), attracts attention by this feature. She came to Christ while he was reclining at table. She had sinned. Still she loved. Here were Christ's feet hanging over the table's edge, while Christ reclined. As he was talking, behold this woman bending over them, her hot tears raining on them, and she busy wiping off the tear-drops with her hair, and kissing them, anointed them with costly ointment. She loved, and therefore evidenced it by deeds. Her love, blossoming into action, won Christ. He saw that she loved. Perhaps love had led her astray at first. No matter. Love she possessed, and love she desired to lavish on some object worthy of her regard. That object she discovered in Jesus. She took her alabaster-box of precious ointment, and went after him. She enters the Pharisee's house; it may have been the house where she had fallen. The Pharisee seemed to know her character, and so he said, "This man, if he were a prophet, would have known who and what manner of woman this is that toucheth him, for she is a sinner." Christ did not at once recognize the suspicion, but supposing the case of the two debtors, and having obtained from Simon the declaration, that the one would love most who was forgiven most, turned upon him the force of the logic, by saying, "Seest thou this woman? I entered into thine house, thou gavest me no water for my feet, but she both washed my feet with tears, and wiped them with the hairs of her head. Thou gavest me no kiss; but this woman, since the time I came, hath not ceased to kiss my feet. My head with oil thou didst not anoint; but this woman hath anointed my feet with ointment. And he said to the woman, *Thy faith hath saved thee; go in peace.*"

Let woman's work be regarded as a work of charity by man, and the larger portion of women will be satisfied. The servant finds pleasure in service, when the obligation is recognized as a debt not to be paid for in money.

No wife would do what she is compelled to perform, or suffer what she is compelled to endure, for her board and clothes. It is when man refuses to give her more than these, she revolts. Man never won woman to leave her single life and her home comforts to enter his house as a helpmeet by a consideration of the work to be done. It was not in the contract. He talked then of love, of companionship, of help. The other was in the bond by mutual consent, but it was regarded as beneath their notice to talk about it. Her nature yearned for love, and lives on love.

Now, when a man forgets that love, companionship, and the thousand attentions which sweeten and brighten life, are due to his wife, and when he lifts up the drudgery and the slavery of life into prominence, and tells her that she is only fitted to hold a menial place, he insults, if he does not destroy the woman, and degrades himself. On the other hand, let a woman refuse to be influenced by this law of charity, and she becomes a curse instead of a blessing, a hinderance instead of a helpmeet.

It is a very common complaint that a good servant is difficult to find. Some are slovenly, some are dishonest, while those who are both able and truthful, are pronounced intolerable, frequently because of their impertinence. All can understand the reason. The servant has no interest in her employer who refuses to *give* anything. The servant works for so much money. "As to rights, privileges, and perquisites, it is not unfrequently either a battle or a sort of armed treaty between kitchen and parlor." Many will admit this, and will forget or ignore the cause. Listen to the servants' story, and you will find them complaining of the stinginess, or tyranny, or selfishness of the employer.

Let the law of charity rule both employer and employed, and behold the change. The mistress recognizes her weight of obligation to a good and faithful domestic. She feels that her services are beyond price, invaluable to her. The effect is seen at once. The sluggish step is quickened. Love takes the place of indifference if not of dislike, and the relations of friendship are at once recognized. No mistress has a right to expect that her servants will be bound to her by the ties of friendship, if she manifest no friendly feeling for them; or that they will become devoted to her interests, if she take no interest in their welfare. The law of mutual dependence must be recognized and obeyed. God is love. God loves. Therefore, it is a pleasure to love and serve God. It is a pleasure to serve whoever is appreciative and lovable. It is a task to serve those who are unappreciative and unlovable. At the same time a Christian servant has no right to slight her work, or be unfaithful, because of the harshness or unkindness of her employer. Live for God, and serve Christ in serving well those by whom you are employed, and you will not lose your reward on earth nor in heaven. Trusty and true, your services will become of immense importance, and doors to usefulness will open before you because of the superintending care of Him who is too wise to err and too good to be unkind. Let not woman dislike the term *service* or *servant*. Christ honored it by becoming the servant of all, and made it honorable by commanding that he who would be chief must serve, and by his service rise.

Woman sometimes revolts because her work is classed under the head of *domestic*, and yet this is the chief characteristic that must distinguish it. That is, her work must have a look homeward, whether she toils in the store or factory or printing-office or kitchen. Somehow the stream of love must sing as it goes babbling by, "Home, home, there is no place like home," else woman fails in her life-work.

Her education must fit her for a home and for home work. Let a man learn that he married a toy, a plaything, a lay figure, useful only for the purposes of exhibiting his taste in jewelry and dress, who desires to be petted and fondled, to be caressed and flattered, but who is incapable of doing anything to contribute to his happiness at home or to his influence abroad, and he comes to feel that she is an encumbrance. If he clings to the old love, and cherishes the old conviction, he learns to treat his wife as a plaything, and to forget her as a helpmeet. He thinks of her as of a toy, which may be used or cast aside at pleasure. She knows and feels the lack of his love. If she becomes dissatisfied, and refuses to make the effort to become a helpful wife and a loving companion, or to be influenced by the law of charity; if she determines to seek happiness in obtaining the admiration of others, which once unwittingly came from her husband; then is she probably ruined, and becomes a "body of death" fastened to one who looks forward to the grave as a refuge and a release, or who finds in the society of other women that pleasure which is denied him at home. Perhaps nothing is more disgusting than to see an empty brain hidden behind a pretty face, or an empty heart concealed beneath costly drapery. A woman who is handsome and is illiterate, who is incapable of speaking entertainingly, is far more homely than a plain face in front of a well cultivated intellect; and a plain dressed woman, with a heart full of love, is to be preferred to a splendidly dressed form which is destitute of soul. Jewels, laces, and silks are not a fit dress for a corpse, and yet a heartless woman is to a man who knows her as soulless as an inanimate body coffined for the tomb. Having thus briefly considered the necessity of linking woman's work and mission together, let us define her work, and consider what is her mission.

Woman has work to do. Though idleness does not destroy her as it does a man, yet it does not become her. Merely to display her charms for the admiration of others cannot be the destiny of one created with a woman's hand and head, and endowed with woman's soul. From the nature of the case, her work should be womanly in its character; that which is within doors rather than without; which belongs to the ornamental rather than to the mechanical. There is no sense in woman's working in the field while man measures tapes or counts thimbles, or in his doing other in-door work for which woman's light touch renders her better qualified. When we look at women who have become coarse in the expression of their features, and ungainly in form and movement, through the weight of their daily toil, we see the folly of those who would make the woman the equal, or the rival, instead of the helpmeet of man; and feel indignation that, since many of our women must earn their own livelihood, we have not a more natural division of labor, which would assign to man the heavier, and to woman the lighter kinds of work. As woman's faith blesses as well as saves her; it is essential that her work be linked in some way to the exercise of faith, and to the unfolding of love. For the character of the work exerts an influence upon woman's body as well as upon her soul. If you will contrast the looks of a happy housewife or domestic with the looks of a majority of the faces that are seen in factories, the truth of the position taken will be abundantly sustained. It matters not so much where the roots of woman's life-work grow, if up through it all, and above it all, the vine may twine its tendril, and send forth its flower, and yield its fruit. For this cause the love of Christ and the hopes of a Christian life seem so essential to her growth and development, that it is almost impossible to write of a happy, contented woman, without describing a woman whose faith in Jesus has regenerated and disinthralled her. Love is the prime requisite to successful endeavor on a woman's part to be her husband's true helpmeet; and so, in discharging the duties incident to a life of toil, woman must be soothed and sustained in her tasks by the joys of a Christian life. Hence the ruin wrought in shops and factories, in stores, and homes where Christ is cast out, and where the bliss of high and holy living is denied.

Woman's mission is to be inferred from a consideration of the wants of man. Created to be a helpmeet for man, it is essential, if we would determine her mission, that we ascertain for what purpose man needs her influence.

God declared, "It is not good for man to be alone," and woman was brought to him as a companion, to charm his life, to prolong it by sharing it with him. Her vocation, by birth, is a vocation of love. To be his helpmeet, not his rival; not to increase, but to lighten, or to support him, under his cares; to recognize him as the immediate object of her existence, instead of fancying that he was formed to wait on her; this is the end for which God has called her into being. As has been said, "This representation may not satisfy the ambition of some, who do but degrade themselves by aspiring to occupy a position for which they are neither intended by God nor qualified by nature,—even as men and angels fell when they sought to become as gods,—but in reality it tends to woman's elevation; and, as the whole history of Christianity doth show, where its truth is most recognized and relied upon, there woman is happiest and greatest."

The word "mission," as applied to woman, refers to the purpose for which she was created and brought to man. In considering her mission, we are safe in avowing that woman found her mission, 1. At home. Her mission is in the home. Her training must fit her for the home, whether she serves as a wife or as a domestic. Her life is a success when she makes home a pleasure and a joy to those to whom the home properly belongs. It is for this reason that there is deep concern on the part of many thoughtful minds because the drift of the times is against educating women for the home. Of the women who are compelled to earn their own subsistence many prefer the factory and the store to the work in the family, and, as a result, there are large numbers of young women who cannot make a loaf of bread or cook a meal, who would not hesitate to become wives of working-men, who expect to find in them a helpmeet in building a home like that which blessed their childhood. The result is dissatisfaction and recrimination, leaving the wife for the club, and turning from the joys of the home to the revel of jovial companions.

The same is true of the class of young ladies who know something of music, vocal and instrumental. They can dance. They have studied drawing sufficiently to be able to sketch a few flowers and figures. Perhaps they can speak French and translate German. They know in what position to sit, and how to move gracefully. All very well these things in their places, and fitted to increase the charm of manner when the eyes are lighted up by the informing soul; not undeserving notice either in their influence upon man, when they are accompanied by something better, for, amid all the weighty cares of life, he is sometimes in the mood when such things do please; but sadly over-estimated when they are made the sole substance and end of a woman's education. They might nearly all be done by a being without a soul. They do nothing to draw out the noble qualities of her deep womanly nature. They leave her altogether unfitted for her peculiar mission of a wife and mother.

Now, there are times when a woman, despite her imperfect education, acquires after marriage the knowledge which fits her for the duties appertaining to wifehood. But where nature yields to such training, the woman fails both in filling her sphere and in fulfilling her mission, and falls beneath her true position as the helpmeet of man. How bitter his disappointment, who, having been smitten by these gewgaw attractions, and having put faith in the mother of the child that with this outward attraction she had corresponding qualifications to fill the home with helpful counsel and sustaining sympathy, when he comes to find that, instead of a *wife*, he has married a plaything, and that his children are being committed to the care of a helpless, unformed companion, rather than to the guidance of a true and noble wife.

A proper conception of woman's mission as the helpmeet of man would tend greatly to her elevation. A man who knows for what woman has been made, and what advantage he should look for from the woman whom he calls wife, will not select a mere toy as the partner of his life; and when woman properly recognizes her place, mothers will not be content to give their daughters, nor will daughters be ambitious, or even content to receive only such a training as fits them for amusing or pleasing man in his playful hours, but leaves them altogether unfit to be his companion under the weightier cares and graver concerns of life.

Let it be understood that woman's life and labor, mission and work, point ever homeward, and whether she serve in the store or shop, in the factory or in the home, she will be ready, whenever God's providence opens the way, to make home bright for another, because it has been made bright for herself. In her reading, in her planning, in her waking dreams and in her night visions, let her live to make her own home joyous, and she will not live in vain. To do this successfully in the future, she must make home bright and beautiful in the present. It is the girl, whose hand is skilful in the home, who is prized as a companion, because of the substantial linked with the ornamental. The same is true of a man. Talent, genius even, is valueless unless it can earn bread. There must be something to make home pleasant with, which it is the duty of man to provide, else woman finds it hard to do her work or fulfil her mission. This does not disparage woman. Her intellect should not be regarded as inferior to man's because it differs from his. Her mind is formed for a distinct work and sphere, just as truly as is her body. In that sphere she is endowed with faculties superior to that of man. Here she has her requital: here she proves herself mistress of the field, and employs those secret resources which might be termed admirable, if they did not inspire a more tender sentiment, both towards her, and towards God, who has so richly endowed her. "Her practical survey, equally sure and rapid; her quick and accurate perception; her wonderful power of penetrating the heart in a way unknown and impracticable to man; her never-failing presence of mind, and personal attention on all occasions; her numerous and fertile resources in the management of her domestic affairs; her ever ready access and willing audience to all who need her; her freedom of thought and action in the midst of the most agonizing sufferings and accumulated embarrassments; her elasticity,—may I say her perseverance,—in spite of feebleness; her tact to practise it, were it not instinctive; her extreme perfection in little things; … her incomparable skill in re-awakening a sleeping conscience, in re-opening a heart that has long been closed; in fine, innumerable are the things which she accomplishes, and which man can neither discern nor offset without the aid of her eye and hand. Thus, mentally as well as physically, is she predestined for a work and sphere different from those of her stronger companions. And, as everything is beautiful in its place and season, so is woman most beautiful and useful when, like a modest flower, she blooms in the privacy for which her nature fits her, and perfumes, with the fragrance of her character, the hallowed precincts of home."[A] "No man," says Mr. Jay, "was ever proof against the kindness of a sensible woman; but where, in all history, can an instance be produced in which an ascendency over him has been obtained by forwardness, scolding, and strife for preeminence? No wife has such influence with, or even such control over, her husband, as

"'She who never answers till her husband cools,
Or, if she rules him, never shows she rules;

Charms by accepting, by submission sways,
Yet has her humor most when she obeys.'"

[Footnote A: Woman's Sphere and Work, by Rev. Wm. Landels, D.D., London.]

2. Woman's mission is social as well as domestic. The domestic part of her life is the garden, in which the seed is planted, which brings forth the flower of social joy. A woman who is the soul of a beautiful home is a power in society. No matter what her talents may be, let it be known that she is a slattern at home, and she is without influence. The pen may serve as a feather to adorn her social life, but it looks mean when the use of it causes the neglect of the needle.

Woman may be a secret power in the home. She may make home attractive to the refined and cultured, and thus prove to be the magnet attracting to herself and to her fireside those gifted sons and daughters, the scintillations of whose genius and the dissemination of whose beautiful thoughts make the home luminous with a light which is inextinguishable. The influence of such a woman over her children and over the young cannot be overestimated.

"Such a sphere, so far from being insufficient to satisfy a true woman's ambition, is well fitted, by its tremendous responsibilities, to excite her fears. There is not one, perhaps, which a human being can occupy, on which hang more stupendous issues. Though less public, it is still more potential than man's."

The influence of a true woman cannot be confined to the home. Home is the fountain, and the world gladly furnishes channels for the diffusion of her influence. In promoting the cause of reform, in alleviating the woes of the unfortunate, in carrying forward the cause of temperance, in ministering to the sick, either as a nurse or a physician, in using her pen to delight and guide the thoughts of the young and old along the garden paths of her own loving life, thick with the blossoms of hope, and made glorious by deeds of charity,—in these, and in numberless other ways, woman, finding her throne in the house, is welcomed as a ruler in the world.

For woman there is a felt a necessity which should send her forth as a missionary to those like herself in everything but blessings. Think of our large factory towns, where women are congregated by hundreds and thousands. Let it be remembered that there is something unnatural in all this. Woman was made for man, for home, for love. Separate her from them all, herd her with her kind, subtract from her the incentive to endeavor, leave her mind to brood in fancy, to welcome unholy aspirations and degrading thoughts to her soul, and you leave her to prey upon herself. Let woman see to it that reading-rooms for women be established in our factory towns, that their boarding-houses be warmed and rendered inviting, that the talented be encouraged to exertion, and that tidiness and neatness be made an incentive for all, and woman will do a work of immeasurable importance,—a work on which God's blessing will rest,—and those who toil to accomplish it will obtain an abundant reward from Him who declares, "Inasmuch as ye did it to one of the least of these, ye did it unto me."

In the cause of Reform woman's help is needed. From the earliest commencement of the temperance movement, appeals, arguments, and expostulations have been addressed by earnest reformers to woman, because it was felt that on any great social question the power of woman to help, or to hinder, was all-important. When it is remembered that woman is the greatest sufferer from the vice of intemperance, that she regulates the customs of society, it is apparent that she should seek to abolish bad, and promote good customs. More than others she trains the young and builds up character, and therefore she should, by example and precept, implant such habits as may be not only a safeguard in childhood and youth, but become fixed as moral principles in those she has reared, when the responsibility arrives; because of these, we find reasons in abundance why woman must help, or aid cannot reach the imperilled and undone.

Again: Woman needs help. Addison well said, "Women are either the best or the worst of human beings." The very feelings which, rightly directed, prompt her to soar even to the apex of the pyramid of human virtue, warped from their right exercise, precipitate her to the lowest and most grovelling depths of human vice. Is woman intemperate, she differs from man in the gratification of her appetite. He seeks the social club. Woman seeks retirement, and drinks alone and apart. Her appetite, from this very cause, becomes unmanageable. Men will stop drinking, oftentimes, when the open bar is closed. Woman, with an appetite formed, drinks the more, because she drinks in secret. Because of this fact, woman is in peril if she form an appetite for strong drink.

Woman as a Mother has work to do as a teacher. "We hear a great deal about education in the present day; but," said Mrs. Ellis, "my strong impression is that there will have to come a teaching out of the mother's heart and life,—herself being taught of God,—such as alone can save us as a nation and a people from falling from our high material prosperity into a condition of moral degradation, which it is terrible to contemplate." Such being the case, every woman should ask, What have I done in those opportunities which God gave me with the young? What did I pour into that open heart and mind? Was my influence for Christ or against him? Which way did I point out to those uncertain feet? Who can estimate a mother's influence! There is a power in a mother's love greater than any other human power,—a power to suffer, to serve, and to save; a power which many waters cannot quench, and which is stronger than death. As she leads, the broodlings will follow. Does she sanction card-playing, theatre-going, dancing, and what are called innocent recreations, or does she set herself against them, and turn the thoughts of her children to books that treat of science, of philosophy, and of religion? Upon the answer to this question the future of children and the young depends. Many a boy has been checked in a career of shame by a mother's sad look; many have been encouraged by a mother's smile. God help women to know how to use their power for home, for woman-kind, for man-kind, for country, and for God!

"No one has such power over a river as he who stands near its source. No one has such power over the tree as he who plants and tends it while yet it is a pliant sapling. And no earthly power is to be compared with that which, humanly speaking, determines the course and destiny of an immortal soul. Under God the mother is the first guardian of the child's eternal interest. It is from the mother, who moves constantly among her little ones, much more than the father, whose vocation necessitates his absence from home, and prevents his being much in their presence, that children receive their bias. Her gentle hand gives to our ductile natures the impress which we wear through life; her loving voice awakens in the soul those sweet echoes which never cease to sound; and her look and manner fill the mind with images which haunt our memory until our dying day."

"O, Mother! sweetest name on earth;
We lisp it on the knee,
And idolize its sacred worth
In manhood's ministry."

A mother's hand gave us our first welcome, and hers was the last we grasped in our farewell. She is the nurse of both of our childhoods; the queen of the home, and the friend of the heart.

"And if I e'er in heaven appear,
  A mother's holy prayer,—
 A mother's hand and gentle tear,—
 That pointed to a Saviour here,
  Shall lead the wanderer there."

Woman's mission is religious. Christ recognized her as a helpmeet, as a comforter, and a companion. Woman ministered to him with delight, and gladly made a resting-place for him in the quiet retreat of the home in Bethany. He recognized her faith as an element of strength, which saves her when properly exercised. The spiritual life of woman is her glory. We think of the woman who had sinned looking in love and faith on Jesus, bathing his feet with her tears, and wiping them with her hair, kissing and anointing them, with a feeling akin to devotion. The Magdalene, delivered of her seven demons, because of her devotion to Christ, and the triumph won by her faith, achieved a position which, in the regards of the church, is equal to that held by the Mother of our Saviour.

Woman's daily life is to her spiritual life what the debris of the stream is to the water-lily that floats upon the surface. What cares the servant girl of Rome for the place where she toils? The cathedral, and the wonderful pictures that hang upon its walls, are her glory and pride. Look at her toil from that stand-point, and she becomes a helper in the estimation of the world that cannot be ignored. We have said woman's work is a work of charity. Satan has warped the truth and wielded it against Christ; but as it is wrong to give up a good tune because bad men sing it, so we must not give up a truth because Satan takes advantage of it. This work of charity,—of giving up for others, of denying self for another's advantage, of abandoning comfort to assuage another's grief,—so wonderfully illustrated by a Florence Nightingale, and by women quite as worthy in our own land, whose presence in the hospitals was like a benediction from God, and whose presence in our homes, in our churches, beside the sad and sorrowing everywhere, is proof that woman has a mission which she alone can fill, and a work which she alone can perform. "And now abideth faith, hope, and charity, and the greatest of these is charity." Man has faith, he has hope; but he lacks, to a large extent, in the charities which come to woman as gifts of God, because of which Christ employed her as an agency to win men back to faith in God. In the sick chamber she moves with step noiseless as falling snow-flakes, and speaks in a voice soft as an angel's whisper. Her touch is so gentle that it soothes the sufferer, and her sympathy is more precious than rubies. On this account she is man's first and last solace. Suffering never appeals to woman in vain. "I never addressed myself," says Ledyard, "in the language of decency and friendship to woman, whether civilized or savage, without receiving a decent and friendly answer. With man it has often been otherwise. In wandering over the barren plains of inhospitable Denmark, through honest Sweden, frozen Lapland, rude and churlish Finland, unprincipled Russia, and the wide-spread regions of the wandering Tartar, if hungry, dry, cold, wet, or sick, woman has ever been friendly to me, and uniformly so; and, to add to this virtue,—so worthy of the appellation of benevolence,—these actions have been performed in so free and kind a manner, that if I was dry, I drank the sweet draught, and if hungry, ate the coarse morsel, with a double relish." Park, and many other travellers, bear similar testimony.

"Woman all exceeds
In ardent sanctitude, in pious deeds;
And chief in woman charities prevail,
That soothe when sorrow or desire assail;
Ask the poor pilgrim on this convex cast,—
His grizzled locks, distorted in the blast,—

Again. We are impelled to seek wisdom from God, because we seek for it in vain elsewhere. As to how the ballot is to help woman, even its advocates give us no light. Whether it is proposed to lighten by its aid the penalties, and do away with the ruin of the fall, we are left in doubt.

If we give to woman the ballot, shall the equality which woman lost, when she ate of the forbidden fruit, be restored, and shall she be made again the equal of man? Shall the sorrow in child-bearing be removed? Can housework, or the duties of motherhood, and wifehood, and sisterhood, be met and discharged by the use of the ballot?

These are questions which deserve to be answered. It is patent to every one that this attempt to secure the ballot for woman is a revolt against the position and sphere assigned to woman by God himself. It is a revolt against the holiest duties enjoined upon woman. It is an attempt to reorganize society upon a new basis; to change the relations of men and women; to secure the millennium by a vote, and by majorities to do away with the rule of God. The Bible declares that the headship of the house devolves on man. Man is lawgiver. Woman is not slave: she is helpmeet; the sharer of man's joys and sorrows; the light of his home, if there be any light in his home; the solace of his life, if his life have solace; the mother of his children, if children there be. Now, as then, woman, in her natural state, before she makes the attempt to unsex herself, and render herself a monster, finds it in her nature to look to man as lawmaker, and expects to submit to his rule in the home. We do not say that all women submit cheerfully to this rule, for there are some who do not. But when this is the case, from the nature of things, happiness takes its flight, the marriage-bed is defiled, woman becomes an outlaw in her heart, and the two bound together by a chain rather than by the silken cord of love, are candidates for a peaceable divorce or a continuous battle.

The advocates of the ballot for woman hope through its aid to secure an overthrow of this rule, or escape from this so-called bondage. They demand a change in public sentiment regarding the sphere woman is to fill, securing to her an equality before the law, in representation, in privileges, and in wages.

In other words, there are women who hope and expect to do away with the disabilities incident to the female portion of the community, and by education and culture, obtain for woman this same strength, this same ability to study, to think, to work, and to plan, that is enjoyed by man. In short, some believe that a woman can be so changed that she can, for all practical purposes, get on without man's help or protection.

Against this revolutionary scheme we protest, because, by a reference to the Word of God,[A] we find reasons for believing that it is in the constitution and nature of woman, with some slight modifications, to occupy the place assigned her in this land, where Christian influence unites with the better instincts of humanity in lightening her burdens, smoothing her pathway, and filling her lap with the tributes of manly regard.

[Footnote A: I am aware that this sneer is often made: "The same class oppose us who defended the divine right of slavery." This is untrue so far as I am concerned. I was second to no man in condemnation of slavery, because the Bible condemned it. That one utterance, "God hath made of one blood all nations of men for to dwell on all the face of the earth," was the seedling out of which liberty, equality, and fraternity grew. Liberty was won because of the faith, and prayers, and efforts of a God-believing and a Christ-loving church. Their prayers and their faith girded the nation with strength, and their prowess, aided by those who followed their lead, secured victory.]

I.

The Scriptural Argument.

To state our faith more definitely, we believe that in Eden woman enjoyed an equality with man; that she took advantage of her privilege, and, transgressing the law of God without consulting her husband, proved treacherous to her high trust, opened the gate of perdition to the enemy of souls, and brought upon man and the race the curse consequent upon sin, and the ruin wrought by the fall. In consequence of this, God pronounced a curse upon her; gave her sorrow in child-bearing, as he gave to man fatigue in toil; changed the relations hitherto subsisting between man and woman, and compelled her to live henceforth in another; to sink her own individuality, and merge it in that of her husband. This is the language. Unto the woman he said, "I will greatly multiply thy sorrow and thy conception; in sorrow thou shalt bring forth children, and thy desire shall be to thy husband, and he shall rule over thee." This is her portion of the curse. This portion endures. Man from that moment became ruler. The wife's desire was to the husband, so that whatever she desires is naturally referred to him. He became adviser, lawmaker and head. The right or wrong of God's action it does not become us to discuss. It is right because God did it. Dispute the right who will, but the curse lives. The serpent crawls on his belly and eats dust. The wife has sorrow in conception; her desire is to her husband, and he rules her; and man, by the sweat of his brow, eats his bread.

But, says some one, did not the coming of Christ change the status of woman, and place her again on the same equality which she enjoyed when Adam led the beautiful Eve to her nuptial bower, and found it impossible to exist without what the poet describes as

>"Thy likeness, thy fit help, thy other self,
>Thy wish exactly to thy heart's desire?"

If we have not mistaken the relations subsisting even in Eden between the original pair, woman was not the ruler even there. Milton has truthfully said,—

>"For well I understand in the prime end
>Of Nature her the inferior, in the mind
>And inward faculties which most excel,
>In outward, also, her resembling less
>His image who made both, and less expressing
>The character of that dominion given
>O'er other creatures; yet when I approach
>Her loveliness, so absolute she seems,
>And in herself complete, so well to know
>Her own, that what she wills to do or say
>Seems wisest, virtuousest, discreetest, best:
>All higher knowledge in her presence falls
>Degraded; wisdom in discourse with her
>Loses discountenanced, and like folly shows;
>Authority and reason on her wait,
>As one intended first, not after made
>Occasionally; and to consummate all,
>Greatness of mind and nobleness their seat

Build in her, loveliest, and create an awe
About her, as a guard angelic placed."

With woman, as God made her, we are not acquainted. Glimpses of her pristine beauty, and characteristics of her former excellence, shine forth; but sin has marred the original picture, and defaced the model fashioned by the Creator's hand. The ruin wrought by the fall brought Christ to earth. He opened a way back to Eden—not on earth, but in heaven. The curse remains. The race is under it, because sin is in the world. The law, formed after the fall, is the expressed will of God. Christ did not come to do away with it, but to fulfil it. Then, as now, it was a law of love, of good will, of peace. When Christ came, woman's condition was deplorable. She was the abject slave of man in nearly all the world. Yet Christ made no attempt to break down their original arrangements. He knew that without a change in woman herself, no external changes in her condition could be of any benefit to her. He recognized the great fact that she herself must be educated to a better life, that she must have a character which in itself would command respect, and make her worthy of a higher place and a larger liberty. Truly has it been said, "Institutions, of themselves, can never confer freedom upon a people. They must be free men, capable of liberty, and then they will be able not only to make their own institutions, but keep and defend them also. So the emancipation of woman can be effected only by breaking the bonds of her ignorance, frivolity, and vice. A character must be given her, and then the iron door of her prison-house will open to her of its own accord, and she will find that the angel of liberty has been leading her forth indeed." In this direction Jesus labored. Paul, in his Epistles, gave emphasis to the teachings of the Old Testament, and so he wrote, "Let your women keep silence, in the churches, for it is not permitted them to speak; but they are to be in subjection, as the law also says; and if they will to learn anything, let them ask their husbands at home; for it is a shame for women to speak in the church,"—I Cor. xiv. 34, 35.

Against this command many arguments have been brought to bear, and despite this apostolic command, some women insist upon their right to preach. It is a significant truth, that whoever does this, enters upon a conflict with public sentiment born of God, and subjects herself to terrible mortification. The refusal of lending Universalist divines to share the exercises of an ordination with a woman, illustrates this principle. The recognition given to man as the head of the household, involves the loss of woman's individuality, and of her right to a support. It opens a window to life, and shows why our higher nature revolts against woman being compelled to labor in the field. That is man's place, and the labor elevates him. It degrades a woman. The praises of agricultural toil for man find a place in song and story; but labor in the field is destructive of womanhood, of motherhood, and of wifehood.

We have seen that the Scriptures declare, 1. That it is not well for man to be alone. He is not complete until woman is joined to him in marriage. 2. Woman was made for man. Manliness is an attribute that belongs to man; it disgraces a woman. To be womanly, is the noblest tribute that can be paid to woman; but it disgraces a man, because God, the Creator, placed this characteristic within the heart and soul and nature, just as he gave a difference of nature, mould, and form, to the outward appearance of man and woman. He made them for a particular purpose, and not for the same purpose. They were not made in the same manner, nor of the same material. If woman be the weaker vessel, she is of the finer mould. God made man in his own image, and woman was created to be his helpmeet.

3. We have noticed the change in the relations which was the product of the curse. Woman in Eden was the source of influence. After it, man became the head, and her desire was unto him.

4. Since the fall, labor has been multiplied to man, sorrow to woman; but such is the kindness of God, that these two facts are sources of perpetual joy in the home. The wife is proud of her toiling husband, the man is tender of his suffering wife; and in the bliss of childhood happiness both find their reward.

These statements shrine all the facts of the separate histories of man and woman. It were easier to change earth to water, and sea to land, than it is to make a womanly woman consent to appear manly. Her God made her a woman. It is not a fault. It is a glory. The bird that skims the wave would not exchange places with the bird that goes to meet the sun; but this is not to bring a charge against the eagle or the swan.

One more truth, and then we will pass to the consideration of the lessons discoverable in woman's nature. All the Scripture requirements, such as refer to the plaiting of the hair, to being uncovered in public, are said to refer to the customs of the East, and not to bind woman in this age of progress. The principle covered by those requirements then, rules now. Paul said, Let not a Christian woman break through any of the restraints of womanhood, and so appear as do the harlots, with uncovered faces and with plaited hair, who mingle freely with men, and are shorn of that modesty and weakness so becoming woman. Woman's right to be a woman implies the right to be loved, to be respected as a woman, to be married, to bring forth to the world the product of that love; and woman's highest interests are promoted by defending and maintaining this right.

There are those who object to the word *service,* and claim that those who take the Bible as authority wish to reduce woman to slavery. No charge could be more absurd; and God's care for woman is manifest, both in the teachings of the Bible and in the constitution of the race. Woman owes to Christianity all she enjoys. Leave her to be subject to the conditions imposed on her by unregenerated manhood or womanhood, and you leave her to become either a thing in society, or else reduce her to a level with the beasts of burden. In old savage and pagan tribes the severest burdens of physical toil were laid upon her. She was valued for the same reason that men prize their most useful animals, or as a means of gratifying sensual and selfish desires. Even in the learned and dignified forms of modern paganism, the wife is the slave rather than the companion of her husband. She is kept apart from him. The education of her mental faculties is neglected. She is not allowed to walk with him; she must walk behind him. She must not eat with him, but eat after he has done, and eat what *he leaves*. She must not sleep until he is asleep, nor remain asleep after he is awake. If she is sitting down, and he comes into the room, she must rise up. She must bow to no other god on the earth besides her husband. She must worship him while he lives, and when he dies she must be burned with him. In case she is not burned, she is not allowed to marry, and is considered an outcast. There is little social intercourse between the sexes, little or no acquaintance of the parties before marriage, and, consequently, little mutual attachment. Women are not allowed to learn to read, because there can be no solid foundation laid for future influence.

Under the Crescent the condition of woman is worse rather than better, for in pagan India she is permitted to share in the hope of religion; but in Mohammedan countries it is a popular tradition that women are forbidden paradise; and it requires some effort for the imagination to conceive how debased and wretched must be the condition of the female sex to originate and sustain such a horrible and blasphemous tradition.

Even in the refined and shining ages of Greece and Rome, where the cultivation of letters and the graces of polished style, the charms of poetry and eloquence, the elegances of architecture, sculpture, painting, and embroidery, the glory of conquest and the pride of national distinction, were unsurpassed, even then and there, woman was but the abject slave of man, the object of his ambition, avarice, lust, and power.

Truly has it been said that nothing more surely distinguishes the savage state from the civilized, the East from the West, Paganism from Christianity, antiquity from the middle ages, the middle ages from modern times, than the condition of woman.

In China, she is used as a beast of burden. The Chinese peasant woman goes to the field with her male infant on her back, and ploughs, sows, and reaps, exposed to all the changes of the weather. In Calcutta, women are the masons, and maybe seen daily conveying their hods of cement, and spreading it on the tops of their houses.

In a country where no European man can labor, where the native rests until compelled by his conqueror to work, seven thousand of these women might have been seen, in 1859, climbing to the edge of ravines, with baskets of stone on their heads, to fill, with these tedious contributions, thousands of perpendicular feet, in order that a railroad might wind among the mountains.

In Australia, she carries the burden which man's indolence refuses; and in Great Britain, the condition of women among the lower classes, revealed by the statistics of her mines and of her manufacturing districts, is such as to make a moralist blush. Behold her, with a strap around her waist, dragging the coal-cart in the mine, and so ignorant, that when asked if she knew Jesus, replied, "He never worked in our shaft."

Do we turn to America, we find that in the providence of God her fortune has been advanced and improved by the extension of the era of free government, and by the diffusion of the principles of the gospel of Christ.

True, in the past, throughout the South, a negro woman worked in the field as a beast of burden; but emancipation and the diffusion of the principles of Christianity changes all this in the South, as it has changed it in Turkey and in the East. The colored man builds for his wife a house, and toils for her in the field or shop, while she keeps the house, and beautifies the sanctuary of the heart.

Now, in all this land, woman's right to be a woman is recognized, and "woman's right to be a man" is opposed, though eloquent orators of either sex may declaim in its behalf. God's law, natural and revealed, is against it. Woman's nature will be woman's nature no longer when she shall desire it.

An illustration of this fact was recently furnished. A female orator had just left the platform for the horse-car. She was tired, and, doubtless, needed a seat. She had been speaking in favor of woman's rights, and had berated the opposite sex for their unwillingness to grant them. Worn out with fatigue, and excited, her lace red, her eyes flashing, she looked around for a seat. The car was full, and among the number sitting down was a workingman.

She spoke so that all could hear her, saying, "You are not gentlemen, or you would not let a woman stand." The workingman looked up, and replied, "Did I not just hear you speak in behalf of woman's rights?" The woman, supposing she had found a friend, replied in the affirmative. "Well," said he, "I will stand up any time, with pleasure, for a housewife or a kitchen girl; but you contend for an equality of rights with men; take it, and stand up among them." The shout of approbation proved that the argument was not on the side of woman. She did not herself believe in the theory advanced. Down in her heart she felt that, because she was a woman, she was entitled to be treated with love and respect, with honor and consideration.

The right which exempts her from certain things which men must endure, *grows out of her right to be a woman*. We feel that it is her privilege and her right to be relieved from the necessity of working in the field, from doing many things which it is manly in man to do.

We do not object to woman's sharing in the toil of the store, the shop, or the factory. Better this than idleness and want; yet there is a reason for pondering the question whether woman is wise in trying to displace man for her own advantage. If any one must be idle, let it be woman, and not man. It has been well said, "There are in Massachusetts over seventy thousand more females than males, and probably twice that number in the State of New York. It is an unnatural condition of things. At the West the number of men greatly preponderates."

"Our young men go off early in life, leaving fathers, mothers, and sisters behind them. The prospect for their sisters to marry, then, is lessened by every emigration." Now, what shall be done in behalf of these thousands of virtuous, educated, and noble girls? The cry is, make them into clerks, and bookkeepers, and bankers, and give them all the employments of men. Think it over. Suppose now we make these girls into clerks in stores and counting-rooms, say ten thousand in Massachusetts, and twenty thousand in New York—don't we displace so many young men; drive them off to the West; prevent so many new families from being established here; take away thirty thousand chances of marriage from these females, and enhance the evil we are trying to remedy?

Is it a blessing to woman to lessen her opportunities of marriage?

Again, a woman can be idle, and not be lost. Whereas man, if left unemployed, runs to mischief, if not to crime.

The history of those manufacturing districts in England, so eloquently described by Charlotte Elizabeth, where woman is preferred because of the cheapness and skill of her labor, proves this position correct. The husband lives in idleness, and has the care of the house. The result is, that comfort and neatness are at an end. The children are reared in crime, in indolence; the men pass their time in drinking and in gambling, prostitution abounds, and the health of the community, socially, physically, mentally, and morally, is destroyed.

On the other hand, enter one of those manufacturing towns where the skilled labor of man is rewarded, and where women keep the house with thrift and care, and you behold order, virtue, and prosperity. This is not poetry. It is fact. It proves that God's laws must be heeded and obeyed. "Marriage," said Gail Hamilton, "is a friendship of the sexes so profound, so comprehensive, that it includes the whole being. The inflow of the divine life,

"'Bright effluence of bright essence increate,'

"blends the man nature and the woman nature into an absolute oneness, which shapes itself ever thereafter into the only perfect symmetry. Thus alone comes humanity in the unity of the faith, and of the knowledge of the Son of God, unto a perfect man, unto the measure of the stature of the fulness of Christ. Thus marriage forever tends to its own annihilation,—not the annihilation of a stream swallowed up in desert sands, but of a river broadening to the boundless sea. The more perfect its substance, the more yielding its form. As it gathers power it diminishes pomp, till, by a pathway which the vulture's eye hath not seen and never can see, marriage itself leads to the land where they neither marry nor are given in marriage.

"Wherever man pays reverence to woman,—wherever any man feels the influence of any woman, purifying, chastening, abashing, strengthening him against temptation, shielding him from evil, ministering to his self respect, medicining his weariness, peopling his solitude, winning him from sordid prizes, enlivening his monotonous days with mirth, or fancy, or wit, flashing heaven upon his earth, and mellowing it for all spiritual fertility,—there is the element of marriage. Wherever woman pays reverence to man,—wherever any woman rejoices in the strength of any man, feels it to be God's agent, upholding her weakness, confirming her purpose, and crowning her power,—wherever he reveals himself to her, just, upright, inflexible, yet tolerant, merciful, benignant, not unruffled, perhaps, but not overcome by the world's turbulence, and responding to all her gentleness, his feet on the earth, his head among the stars, helping her to hold her soul steadfast in right, to stand firm against the encroachments of frivolity, vanity, impatience, fatigue, and discouragement, helping to preserve her good nature, to develop her energy, to consolidate her thought, to utilize her benevolence, to exalt and illumine her life,—there is the essence of marriage. Its love is founded on respect, and increases self-respect at the very moment of merging itself in another. Its love is mutual, equally giving and receiving at every instant of its action. There is neither dependence nor independence, but inter-dependence. Years cannot weaken its bonds, distance cannot sunder them. It is a love which vanquishes the grave, and transfigures death itself into life."

These laws are varied by God's word, and written indelibly upon the nature of man. Surely nothing can be more manifest than that they must be obeyed.

II.

Nature teaches us the Wisdom of adhering to the Divine Plan.

Anatomists tell us that in the embryo skeleton there is a marked difference of general conformation in the two sexes; that in the male there is a larger chest and breathing apparatus, which, affects the whole organization, forming a more powerful muscular system, and producing a physical constitution which predestines him to bold enterprises and daring exploits. The woman, being differently constructed, finds it natural to content herself in the house, removed from the gaze of the world, and from rude contact with its jostling cares.

There is an outside and an inside world. The work of the street, or the shop, or the field, is no more essential to the well-being of the family than is the work performed in the house. God assigned to man the field, or out-door work, and to woman the home and housework. In proportion as men and women fill well their separate spheres, there is harmony and happiness. Man toils, and provides for the wants of his household. Woman toils, and sees to it that the children are well reared, and that the house is well kept. Woman is respected and supported, not in idleness, but in caring for the wants of those committed to her care. The attempt is being made to disregard these natural laws, by those who claim to have outgrown divine legislation, and who have the hardihood to trample upon the laws of nature.

But in vain. When God made our first parents, he made them male and female, and it will not be difficult to believe in the impossibility of the finite being able to undo the work of the Infinite. Each has his and her place, and nothing goes continuously right if husband and wife change places. Keep the positions assigned them by the laws of God and nature, and all will go well.

Give to woman the serious consideration due from every man born of woman's agony, and you build her up in love, endow her with respect, encourage her to cultivate her mind, and to develop the graces of her nature. The mightiest influence which exists upon earth is concealed in the heart of woman. It follows that her elevation and her happiness, her education and usefulness, are objects of deep concern. We have seen that the legislation of Heaven provides for the gratification of the early longing of the soul for companionship in making marriage honorable and love the holiest of instincts.

It is fashionable to talk against an early love. It is wrong thus to do. "Youth longeth for a kindred spirit, and yearneth for a heart that can commune with his own. He meditateth night and day, doting on the image of his fancy." It is the tendency of an early love to inspire youth with grand aspirations and lofty aims. "They that love early, shall become like-minded, and the tempter shall touch them not. They shall grow up, leaning on each other, as the olive and the vine."

It is only when love is scorned, when passion takes its place, when man forgets that the idol of his heart is a probationer of earth like himself, that it is his duty to be chary of her soul, feeling that it is his jewel. It is only when a man ceases to be a man, and becomes a beast, that he can consent, even in thought, to despoil woman of her virtue; to trample upon the sacred instincts of her nobler nature. A real woman will delight to make herself worthy of love. In the advancement of her mind, quite as much as in the adornment of her person, she strives to make herself beautiful as well as lovable. If she forgets her duty, and consents to seem to be what she is not, so that her admirer finds that the appearance which charmed him was not real, then the future of that woman is dark indeed. Her husband will discover, when too late, that "the harp and the voice may thrill him, sound may enchant his ear, but, by and by, the hand will wither, and the sweet notes turn to discord; the eye, so brilliant at even, may be red with sorrow in the morning; and the sylph-like form of elegance must writhe in the crampings of pain."

Naturally the man and woman will recognize the rule of God in the choice of their vocation. He will go abroad, and she will stay at home. He will earn the bread, and she will make it. He will build the house, and she will keep it. The difference between their spheres of labor seems naturally to be this: one is external, the other internal; one active, the other passive. He has to go and seek out his path; hers usually lies close under her feet. Yet, if life is meant to be a worthy one, each must resolutely be trod.

> "When the man wants weight, the woman takes it up,
> And topples down the scales; but this is fixt
> As are the roots of earth and base of all:
> Man for the field, and woman for the hearth;
> Man for the sword, and for the needle she;
> Man with the head, and woman with the heart;
> Man to command, and woman to obey;
> All else confusion."

Woman is not content to remain separate and apart. She will give her love to some object, and desires to repose her faith in some person worthy of her regard. She lives for man. She dresses and studies for him. She acquires knowledge and accomplishments, which are known to please and to allure.

Woman, being by nature dependent, finds it easier to lay hold of the offer of salvation than does man. His independent spirit keeps him back. Woman has only to recognize her dependence upon One higher than man, and in doing this is obliged to do but little violence to her habits of thought and feeling, and no violence at all to such sentiments of independence as stand most in the way of man. Hence men shrink with horror from coming in contact with a godless woman. In their eyes she is monstrous, unreasonable and offensive. Even an utterly godless man, unless he be debauched and debased to the position of an animal, deems such a woman without an excuse. He looks on her with suspicion. He would not intrust his children to her care. Oh happy lot, and hallowed even as the joy of angels, where the golden chain of godliness is entwined with the roses of love, as one of our own poets wrote:—

"O, what is woman—what her smile,
Her lip of love, her eye of light;
What is she if her lip revile
The lowly Jesus? Love may write
His name upon her noble brow,
Or linger in her curls of jet;
The bright spring flowers may scarcely bow
Beneath her step, and yet, and yet
Without that meeker grace, she'll be
A lighter thing than vanity."

Thus wrote N.P. Willis. He felt that a woman, with Christ in her heart, was the *beau ideal* of man. The home is her kingdom, and the heart of husband or brother is her throne. In that sphere her influence is the most potent instrumentality on earth.

Demosthenes declared that by this influence she can in an hour upset the legislation of a year of statesmanship. Her power is, however, through man, not apart from him.

This is the scriptural view. Nowhere do we read of woman as though she had a mission apart from man. We talk of men and forget women. It seems almost impossible to legislate for woman and forget man.

Mankind includes womankind, but womankind does not include mankind.

It may not be complimentary, yet it remains true, that the Scriptures fail to furnish us with a model woman.

Jesus was the model man; but Eve, and Mary, and Rebekah, and Rachel, were model women to none besides those to whom they were given as wives. This, perhaps, is well, for it would be injudicious to try and prove to any man that his wife should differ radically from herself.

III.

Having considered the teachings of the Scripture and of Nature, let us listen to the Voice of Common Sense.

Under this head we hesitate not to declare that the hope of woman lies in the recognition of the laws of God, and the laws of her own higher nature.

Look at the facts. Who demand the ballot for woman? They are not the lovers of God, nor are they the believers in Christ, as a class. There may be exceptions, but the majority prefer an infidel's cheer to the favor of God and the love of the Christian community. It is because of this tendency that the majority of those who contend for the ballot for woman cut loose from the legislation of Heaven, from the enjoyments of home, and drift to infidelity and ruin.

Our wives and mothers do not ask the ballot. Our young ladies do not care even to hear the question discussed. They believe that whatever hinders woman from being the helpmeet of man does her injury. It is claimed that woman needs the ballot to secure equal laws. This claim is urged, because, it is said, women are required to obey laws which they had no share in making. It is a mistaken notion. Woman has had a share in the legislation of the country. Her influence pervades society. Let her be true to temperance, and intemperance is restrained. Let her be true to freedom, and the pulsations of her heart find their way through the entire framework of society. Let her be true to her own glorious nature, and this attempt to unsex and discrown her will meet with the swift and terrible condemnation it deserves.

Another has said, "The Amazons have often been met with the statement, that a large majority of the women do not wish to vote, and would not if they could. The truth of this statement is not denied. The advocates of the ballot confess that many noble women affect a womanly horror of being thought strong-minded," and to offset this tendency they declare it to be the "imperative duty of women to claim the suffrage." "Does this mean that women are to be coerced in this matter? that our mothers, wives, and sisters are to be punished for staying away from the polls? We have never supposed it the imperative duty of every man to vote. And we know that many of the most intelligent and upright do not vote. Such is the inexpressible nastiness of our elections, especially in the larger cities, that men of the cleanest morals think it right to keep away from them. The foulest portions of the men go first, stay longest, and stand thickest at the places of voting. How then will it be when the foulest portion of the women get packed into the same crowd, and drive modesty away by the foulness of their speech and presence? When the aggregate filth of both sexes shall have met together at the polling stations, as it will be sure to do, we hardly think any chaste or modest home-loving woman will go near this stench unless compelled to do so."

It is because this scheme lifts the gate to the increasing wave of corruption and pollution, that we are surprised that so-called statesmen give their countenance to it. Give to woman the ballot, and this country is hopelessly given up to Romanism. The priest loses the man, but he keeps the woman. Give to the priests the control of the votes of the thousands of servants in the great cities, and there is an end to legislation in behalf of the Sabbath, the Bible, and the school system, temperance, or morality.

The right to vote implies the right to rule, to legislate, to go to Congress, and to take the Presidential chair. On this point hear Miss Muloch. "Who that ever listened for two hours to the verbose confused inanities of a ladies' committee, would immediately go and give his vote for a Female House of Congress, or of Commons? or who, on the receipt of a lady's letter of business,—I speak of the average,—would henceforth desire to have our courts of justice stocked with matronly lawyers, or thronged by

"'Sweet girl graduates, with their golden hair?'"

Well has Gail Hamilton said, "How will the possession of the ballot affect in any way the vexed question of work and wages? One orator says, 'Shall Senators tell me in their places that I have no need of the ballot, when forty thousand women in the city of New York alone are earning their daily bread at starving prices with the needle?' But what will the ballot do for those forty thousand women when they get it? It will not give them husbands, nor make their thriftless husbands provident, nor their invalid husbands healthy. They cannot vote themselves out of their dark, unwholesome sewing-rooms into counting-rooms and insurance offices, nor have they generally the qualifications which these places require. *The ballot will not enable them to do anything for which their constitution or their education has not fitted them, and I do not know of any law now which prevents them from doing anything for which they are fitted, except the holding of government offices.* ... What can the ballot do towards equalizing wages, where work is already equalized without affecting wages, as is not unfrequently the case? There are shops of the same sort, on the same street, with male clerks in one and female clerks in another, where the former work fewer hours and receive higher wages than the latter....

Moreover, the question of female clerkship is not yet settled. There are conscientious, intelligent, and obliging shopkeepers, who say that female clerks are not satisfactory. Their strength is not equal to the draughts made upon it. They are not able to stand so long as clerks are required to stand. They have not the patience, the civility, the tact that male clerks have…. All the voting in the world can never add a cubit to a woman's stature."

Woman is not naturally a law-maker. Even in our homes she desires the head of the house to lay down the law. Never shall I forget the influence exerted by the utterance in a convention of Sabbath school teachers. A paper was read, complaining that in a certain Sabbath school there was a lady superintendent, because no man could be found to take the place. In conclusion, the writer said, "We need a man in our town. We have things that wear pantaloons, but we need a man, to give direction to the school, and to attract the nobler and better portion of community." It was an honest declaration, and voiced a truth. Every town, every Sabbath school, every home, needs a man. Women of talent have tried to figure in politics and in the pulpit, but a sorry figure they have made of it.

Think of Miss Anthony and Mrs. Stanton in the train of George Francis Train, perambulating the country in favor of the ballot in Kansas. These are the leaders; but let it not be forgotten that they sided against the ballot for the negro in hopes of getting it for themselves, and proved their utter worthlessness and untrustworthiness by trailing the banner committed to their keeping in the slime of a convention which went for the repudiation of the national debt, the defeat of the party of progress, and for the overthrow of republican liberty. Had woman possessed the ballot, and had the course pursued by the leaders of this movement exercised an influence over the majority, this wonderful victory over the rebellious spirits of the land had not been achieved; but, in its stead, the stars and bars would have resumed their sway, and the stars and stripes, which now kiss the breeze, and greet the rising hopes of uncounted millions, would have been furled in gloom and night.

It is claimed that the ballot will secure for woman social respect. The claim is not well founded. Those who seek it lose social respect, because they step out of the path marked out for them by Providence and by Nature. Woman, in her sphere, is man's good angel and helpmeet; out of it, she is man's bitterest foe and heaviest curse.

There is an instinctive respect for woman in her proper sphere, which is of itself a power superior to any merely conventional position that a woman can build up for herself by her own hands, even through the aid of the ballot.

How natural to see woman waited on by man! Sir Walter Raleigh was praised because he cast his cloak into the mud to save the foot of his Queen from being soiled. As noble acts have been performed by many men, times without number. The uprising of gentlemen in the cars when a tired woman enters with a child; the disposition to lighten her cares and sweeten her joys, is everywhere considered manly.

Education is essential for her. She is the educator of the home, for she is its soul. If one must be ignorant, let it be the man, and not the woman. Many of our most intelligent men have had cultured mothers. Very few sons ever grew to be learned whose mothers cared not for books. This fact is appreciated, and leads us naturally to conclude that if woman lacks social respect it is her own fault. If a woman prefers superficiality to thoroughness; music, drawing, and dress, to a knowledge of housework, an acquaintance with literature, and the endowments of common sense, simply because brainless men are disposed to seek out the effeminate and the frail in preference to the rugged and the well-endowed, then she must suffer the consequences. If a young lady, compelled to toil for support, will prefer the factory or the store, with its hot air and depressing associations, to work in the home, because she hopes in the store or factory to secure the hand and heart of a husband sooner than elsewhere, she must suffer accordingly. But if woman will unite in securing a reform in this direction,—if the pure and the virtuous will say, Such a life as is offered me in the family is in harmony with my future well-being, and I will scorn the allurements elsewhere held out, and fit myself, by study, for companionship with the noble of the land, she will succeed. If woman will respect herself, she will be respected.

It is not by clamoring for rights that have been conferred upon others; it is not by restless discontent, by partisan appeals, by stepping out of her God-given sphere, and by attempting to destroy the network of holy influences by which he ever has surrounded her; it is not by ridiculing marriage and casting scorn on motherhood, that she is to obtain the blessings she courts, but by tranquilly laboring under this heaven-imposed law of obedience. Woman's weakness is transmuted into strength when she opens her nature to the influences of love, and when she consecrates herself to the happiness of others. Then it is she obtains a moral and spiritual power to which man is glad to do homage. Ambition, pride, wilfulness, or any earthly passion, will distort her being. She struggles all in vain against a divine appointment. It is from the soul of meekness that the true strength of womanhood is derived; and it is because it has its root in such a soil that it has a growth so majestic, showering its blessing and fruits upon the world.

It was the sun and the wind that in the fable strove for the mastery; and the strife was for the traveller's cloak. The quiet moon had nought to do with such fierce rivalry of the burning or the blast; but as in her tranquil orbit she journeys round the world, she gently sways the tides of the ocean. Woman's influence resembles that exerted by the queen of night. In the conflicts of life she has little to do; but her influence is felt from the cradle to the grave, and the sphere of it is the whole region of humanity. Woman's worst enemy is he who would cruelly lift her out of her sphere, and would try to reverse the laws of God and of nature in her behalf. They deceive woman who cause her to believe that she will find independence when she abandons the position assigned her by her Creator, and reaches one against which her nature, the interests of society, and the laws of God contend. Woman has her sphere and her work, and she is only happy when she finds pleasure in lovingly, patiently, and faithfully performing the duties and enacting the relations that belong to her as woman. She is not the natural head of society. Man, rough, stern, cold, and almost nerveless, is made to be the head of human society; and woman, quick, sensitive, pliant (as her name indicates), gentle, loving, is the heart of the world. As the heart, she has power. She rules through love, and finds the work set for her to do in the doors opening before her loving nature. She rules through love, and becomes a blessing greater than we can ever acknowledge, because it is greater than we can measure. Let woman take heart. She is not in captivity. The law of service is on her, as it is on man. Much of her service consists in suffering; much of man's consists in toil. Before both there are fields of endeavor, white with beckoning harvests. In literature, in reforms, in ministering to the wants and woes of humanity, in making home more and more like heaven, woman has an open door set before her, which no man will desire to close. Let her enter it and work. There is a law of companionship far deeper than that of uniformity and equality, or similarity —the law which reconciles similitude and dissimilitude, the harmony of contrast, in which what is wanting on the one side finds its complement on the other; for,—

"Heart with heart and mind with mind,
When the main fibres are entwined,
Through Nature's skill,

  May even by contraries be joined
  More closely still."

Such was the exquisite companionship of the sexes as they were represented by our first parents, and such, however they may be momentarily disturbed, they will remain, as the ideal for all the generations of men and women. Let woman repose her trust in man, and then, lifting up her heart, she may sing,—

  "Though God's high things are not all ours,
    'Tis ours to look above;
  All is not ours to have and hold,
    But all is ours to love."

www.ingramcontent.com/pod-product-compliance
Lightning Source LLC
Chambersburg PA
CBHW081159020426
42333CB00020B/2556